THE MATTER OF CONSCIOUSNESS

Story Waters

Limitlessness Publishing

CONTENTS

For Roger

WHEN READING PLEASE TAKE WHAT
RESONATES & LEAVE THE REST

YOUR DREAM STARTS HERE

"I choose to live my most exciting dream."

Your spirit, its dream for this life, and your embodied self all meet within the realization of your infinite freedom to create experience. Your dream is a feeling that unfolds from within you. Or, if you have not yet ventured through the doorway of freely allowing the flow of your feelings, it is experienced as the unfolding of your life in the mirror of external reality.

The face of your dream is the outward manifestation of seeing and knowing yourself clearly. This is to realize that the living of your dream and the experience of your self cannot be divided because you are the living of your spirit's dream. You came here to be yourself — just as you are.

Your dream is to be yourself, and
that carries no obligation to learn or
evolve (though we always do).

Spiritual awakening is the realization that you are free and infinite, even when you are embodied within a mortal life. You are waking up from a dream and realizing that you are the dreamer, not just a character in the dream. This is to meet the experience of your spirit through meeting the freedom of your consciousness. It is felt as grounding your spiritual freedom into your human experience. It is to know there are no obstacles except those you create for yourself by believing that pain and struggle are inevitable.

*Let go of any belief that says your
dream is not for today.*

All that appears to separate you from your dream is a perceptual illusion—*a lie*—that you will transform and release as soon as you see it. The mask of this illusion is recognized through the many names we have given our fears. Face and transform your fears to be free.

*Your physical body is not a cage — it is your
spirit expressing its desire to experience this life.*

We are each much more than the physically incarnate aspect of our being. Release your wounds to experience the freedom of your spirit in ever clearer ways. Our human form is but one face of our infinite state of consciousness. If you allow yourself to enter a wider experience of self—*through the transformation of your fears*—then you will walk into your dreams.

*A free consciousness naturally inhabits
its most passionate idea of life.*

A reality of joyous freedom—*the reality of your creatorship*—is but a realization away. To be free is to live your dream because that is the nature of consciousness within freedom. Living your dream means creating the life you desire, not just passively waiting for it to happen.

This is the life.

The time is now.

Your dream starts here.

CLARIFICATIONS & REFLECTIONS

Your spirit is the non-physical level of consciousness from which you chose to enter into the human experience of individuality. Spiritual awakening is becoming as familiar with your spirit as you are with your physical self. This is most easily understood as the path of learning to live through the guidance of your feelings, instead of through the fear-based wounds within your mind.

You have the ability to be aware of the reality of your spirit —*whether you choose to use that ability or not*—by opening yourself to a more allowing experience of consciousness. Contrary to many of the teachings of religion, the purpose of human existence is not to awaken to your spirit and *"ascend"* to the non-physical state. From the inherent freedom of our eternal spirit, we created the human form because it is precisely what we wanted to experience.

We did not create the human experience as a prison to escape or a hardship to endure.

The idea that reality is a test we must pass—*or a punishment we must submit to*—arose through religion because of its use of fear as a tool of control. Anyone who lives a joyful life that flows from their heart—*regardless of their spiritual beliefs*—is doing what they birthed here to do (even if they die without any belief in an afterlife and a dislike for spirituality).

You are under no obligation or pressure to recognize your spiritual nature—*the innate freedom of your consciousness*—through any particular way or name. Being spiritual does not require you to call it *'spirituality'* or dress it up in *'religious sounding'* words or rituals. You could instead call it *'authenticity'* or *'living consciously with love.'* The choice is yours, and that choice empowers you to shape your spiritual journey as you see fit.

> *You are not here to awaken to your spirit*
> *—although you can choose to—you are*
> *here to live your spirit's dream.*

Our dreams are about joy ... not some idea of an external god.

Our dreams are about love ... not sacrificing who we are.

Our dreams are about the beauty of feeling ... not mental construction based on the accumulation and refinement of knowledge.

The dream in your heart cannot be met through the idea that you *'should'* be spiritual. Joy is met through the realization that we *ALL* intend—*and deserve*—to live in joy. Do not believe in the ideas in this book because you want to be *'more spiritual.'* Believe in *ANY* idea—*no matter where you find it*—that aids you in living your life through a state of joy and appreciation.

GUIDANCE WITHIN

*"I choose to follow the feeling within
my heart above all else."*

Y ou already contain everything you seek. You are
the only person who can ultimately answer your
deepest questions. Do not let any external moral
construct define your boundaries. Do not try to be anyone
or anything other than yourself. Your journey is unique and
special.

*There is nothing to prove, and the
approval of no person—except
yourself—can free you.*

Every person is a teacher of *what they are* and best teaches
what they incarnated to learn. If you write a book, write the
book you have always wanted to read. Write it so you can read
it. Birth into reality what you have always wanted to be there.

Take responsibility for your desires because—*when they are not coming from fear*—they are a powerful part of the guidance from which you create your reality.

Following someone else whose answer feels close to your own may well take you far. However, following them can never bring you to what you seek most. At some point you must stop following others in order to be true to yourself.

The feeling that every fiber of your being yearns for cannot be found within the static nature of knowledge or arrived at like a fixed destination. The feeling you seek is a state of being ... a state of isness.

> *There are many incredible shades of light you can bask in, but the only hue you can completely stand in is your own.*

What you seek is the experience that arises when you learn to fearlessly follow the feeling of guidance that flows through your heart. While you are following someone else—*no matter how wise they may be*—you cannot be following the guidance of your own feelings (because you cannot follow two differing compasses simultaneously).

To be told a wise observation that personally touches you is like receiving the gift of a delicious meal when hungry. To learn to follow your inner guidance is to draw sustenance from the eternally abundant river of potential that is life. When you do this, you will not only discover the nature of abundance, but you will directly experience how the guidance of your feelings flows from a state of unified knowing. The light and joy you feel is the level of shared eternal consciousness that shines from within all.

You are the light that you seek.

It is time to awaken your potential to be and live *all that you are.*

Awaken and live out the dreams that birth from the feeling within your heart.

Trust in your inner guidance, for it will lead you to *'know thyself.'*

The feeling of what you resonate with draws you forward and acts as a guiding light in your life. This is not guidance from your spirit being sent to you — it is you guiding yourself by directly tapping into the feeling of your spirit and using it to determine what you resonate with.

If every person followed the guidance that arises through the feeling of their spirit, then the harmony of spirit would be collectively experienced (because our spiritual guidance —*when felt clearly*—does not conflict). And yet, this guidance is not felt to be coming from a shared place — instead, it is intimately felt to be your own uniquely personal desire for joy, clarity, and awareness.

To allow your feeling of resonance to engulf you—*such that there is no room for doubt or fear*—is to unify with your spirit. In this state, you are open to the experience of freedom through the infinite potential of creation (which is to be constrained only by your imagination).

To focus on living within experiences you resonate with is to focus on your freedom to be.

This is to focus on creating your personal dreams of what can be — these are your hopes for the future that arise in response to the unconditional love and allowance of your spirit meeting the divisiveness and separation of the human experience. Living within experiences you resonate with means actively seeking out and engaging in activities, relationships, and environments that align with your *resonance/inner guidance*, bringing you a sense of joy, fulfillment, and growth.

The most exciting wonders of this world birth from people who follow their inner feeling of how they are different—*such that they arrive at something new*—rather than seeking to refine or perfect what is already known. Seek to embody this fearless state of consciousness to unleash its potential to create the exciting, child-like fantasies that flow freely through your imagination.

Be open to experience and consider the many perspectives this world offers you so that you may better discover the beliefs and practices with which you most clearly resonate. Be open to the world to taste and be inspired by its diversity. However, no matter how dominant a particular source of information or resonance becomes, never stop personally evaluating everything you perceive.

> *To spiritually awaken is to discover your own uniquely personal understanding of what you choose to experience as truth.*

YOUR WIDER
EXISTENCE

*"I choose to meet, know, and
be 'all that I am' through no
longer perceptually dividing my
experience, and thereby myself."*

Your spirit is a creative force within consciousness that exists eternally in a state *of infinite potential/ freedom*. 'Spirit' is the unconstrained experience of consciousness that we each birth from.

Your embodied self is your infinite eternal spirit within a mask of fear and forgetting through which it willingly chooses to have an experience of being mortal and limited. It does this by cloaking itself in the illusion of fear that underpins our experience of individuality — such as feeling *separation/ alienation, attachment/possessiveness, loss/grief, competition/*

superiority, stuck/imprisoned, and *pain/suffering.* These feelings are underpinned by forgetting we are eternal and focusing on our mortality — usually through the lens of fearing death.

While embodied, we experience the infinite potential of our spirit as our imagination — an inner experience through which we taste the reality of our spirit. Because our spirit does not experience itself as separate from anything, it is not capable of feeling loss, wounding, fear, or the pain of struggling to survive.

Our spirit is deeply in love with the vibrancy of physical life and is filled with excitement and eagerness to embrace the challenges of being human. This joy and excitement are not to be feared but met inside of yourself and celebrated as a part of the rich tapestry of human experience.

Many spiritual teachings idealize our spirit while denigrating our humanity; this polarizing action denies how our spirit births our mortal self from its state of infinite freedom.

To judge your human self to be inferior—*because it is neither entirely free nor constantly joyful*—is to create a division within your perception of reality and your experience of self.

As the allowing, loving, and inclusive nature of your spirit becomes clear, it is most easily identifiable as the aspect of you that does not know or experience fear. You will see how your fears—*which you birth with and continue accumulating across your life*—have come to adorn your human self and form an intricate, perceptual cloak. This mask of mortality focuses the unique intention through which your immortal spirit joyfully created your mortal life. Your embodiment is an extension of your spirit and cannot be said to be inferior to it.

*Your mortal self is your spirit looking at itself
within a mirror that focuses and reflects its
infinite nature as a highly focused individual.*

CLARIFICATIONS & REFLECTIONS

Your *mortal self* is an embodied form of your eternal spirit.
Because our physical bodies have a finite lifespan, we perceive
ourselves to be mortal with a beginning and end point in
linear time. As such, our mortal self is experienced as being
both *contained by* and *defined within* linear time and physical
space.

*Your spirit is the founding aspect of your
human experiences of self and consciousness.*

Your spirit exists outside the confines and definitions of
linear time and physical matter—*meaning it exists eternally in
a state of infinite freedom*—and remains accessible to you even
though you are currently embodied. Because your spirit does
not experience fear or separation, it knows itself to be directly
connected to everything in existence. You are not alone; you
are part of a single unified state of consciousness — the source
of all creation.

While embodied, we are largely unconscious of our spirit
despite it being the origin and foundation of our experience.
To spiritually awaken is to become aware of this wider state of
consciousness. This is to know *all that you are* (which includes
your outward experience, your inner emotions and thoughts,
and the unconstrained freedom of your *spirit/imagination).*

Within most organized religions, this unified state of
consciousness is worshiped as God. However, instead
of teaching us how we are an extension of this infinite

consciousness, God is portrayed as a separate, superior, patriarchal state of consciousness against which we are each judged and found to be lacking.

To awaken is to remember that YOU ARE GOD
and the only judgment you face is your own.

You were not forced to incarnate against your will because you have sinned. You are not here because something within you needs to be fixed. *Your mortal self is your spirit incarnate.* Feel empowered by viewing your life as a choice you are willingly making rather than something difficult you must endure or overcome.

Embrace the realization that you want
this mortal experience — no matter
how challenging it may be.

When you divide the world into *'what I love'* and *'what I hate,'* you create a division in your experience of self and your experience of reality — a perceptual divide through which you can feel separate and alone. Let go of the idea that your embodied self is inferior and see yourself as the choice of your infinite spirit to exist as a focused individual.

THE INVITATION BEFORE YOU

*"I choose to take only what resonates
and simply leave the rest."*

You cannot remember what the reality of your spirit is like through the accumulation of knowledge. The experience of your spirit cannot be contained in the linearity of language. What you seek through spiritual awakening is far more than mental. You seek the feeling of resonance that connects your human self with the infinite freedom of your spirit.

While reading this book, whenever you feel the resonance of love in your heart, leave the words behind and unfold the feeling of freedom and limitlessness evoked within you. The full knowing of the freedom of our consciousness is direct —*you must BE IT to know it*—because freedom exists before thought. Words are but *a conduit/a portal/a birth-gate* that, once traveled through, can be discarded, like a caterpillar discards its cocoon.

*All experiences of truth are evolving
because humanity is evolving.*

The spiritual teachings of tomorrow will be different from those of today. In all you discover, take only what resonates and leave the rest. If you cannot resist the urge to judge something being said, then accept the gift of realizing you are prompting yourself to re-evaluate your beliefs.

Anything that pushes an emotional button in you signals you are operating from a limited perspective. Instead of judging yourself for this, open your mind—*and thereby your perception of reality*—to widen your perspective such that you may further embrace your *freedom to be* and live your life without resistance.

*Take what resonates in this book inside of
yourself and use it as a catalyst to create,
discover, and open your own unique perspective.*

These ideas are simply *words on paper* that invite you to feel the wider reality you exist within. Take ownership of your personal interpretation of these invitations to spiritual states of perception by recognizing that your understanding of each sentence is uniquely your own. If you experience transformation through reading this book, know it is your own doing, your own choice, and your own creation.

*Your personal interpretation is the
key to your spiritual growth.*

These words are a creative fuel for you to explore the potential of your choice, your empowerment, and your change. How these ideas blossom is purely *by you, for you,* and *of you.* These words have not been written to encourage you to duplicate some homogeneous ideal; they are a catalyst and fuel for your own unique self-creation — your choice to see and be *all that you already are.*

CLARIFICATIONS & REFLECTIONS

Resonance, in the context of spiritual growth, is a positive feeling of *attraction to* or *connection with* the object of your perception. It is not just about positive, affirming thoughts that flow through your mind but more the deeper, wordless, feeling-based state that you experience through your heart (with your heart being a metaphor for your capacity to feel). This feeling-based resonance is what guides you to make decisions that align with your *spirit/dream,* instilling you with confidence and a *sense/knowing* of being guided in your choices.

The feeling of resonance is particularly useful—*and powerful*—when considering each of the options available within a choice you are making. By choosing what your heart resonates with most—*rather than what your mind tells you is logically the best option*—you are choosing from the knowing of your spirit. As such, your choice is based on its incredible breadth of perception as well as its state of fearless allowance.

> *Fearless allowance is the state of being open and accepting of all possibilities without being swayed by fear or doubt.*

Expression through language, mental learning, and teaching are powerful, transformative experiences. However, deep within the experience of feeling—*and not your thoughts*—you will discover the direct experience and knowing of freedom ... the state your spirit exists within. This is not to say that you should disregard or demonize your thoughts, but it is to understand them as a reflection of your feelings. Your *feelings/emotions* are a powerful form of understanding which can lead you to the direct experience of freedom your *wider consciousness/spirit* exists within.

Everyone carries personal, self-limiting beliefs from their upbringing. These can be recognized and liberated from the resistance of fear, such that you can reconnect with the states of freedom and joy they have separated you from. Exploring these divisive beliefs has not been a mistake. The experience of their transformation is a powerful step in your unique path of awakening.

Through your experience of the incredible amount of information available in the human experience—*more than you could learn in a thousand lifetimes*—see how accumulating information is like collecting more and more jigsaw pieces for a puzzle with no edges. Although this can be a fun game, recognize that if you allow your feeling of resonance to guide you, you will quickly lead yourself directly to the information and experiences that will most benefit you.

Information is not an end-destination in the exploration of our personal truth. Using your inner feeling of guidance allows you to let information flow freely through your mind — without you needing to accumulate or possess it.

> *Information is only ever valuable as a stepping stone to achieve deeper states of feeling/emotional realization.*

TO KNOW LOVE IS TO KNOW FREEDOM

"I choose to feel my being through the expression of unconditional love, which I express through sharing my appreciation of those I love, rather than sacrificing myself for them."

L ove is not an action you do to someone — it is a feeling that arises when you perceive them without fear or judgment. Unconditional love, in its purest form, is a state of appreciation that is all-encompassing. It allows no room for any thought of trying to improve or change what you are appreciating.

When you love someone unconditionally, you love them as they are without seeking to change them.

Unconditional love is powerful because it values the person without any hidden agenda. This is to simultaneously feel love and the feeling of being loved.

Recognizing love as a feeling—*rather than an action*—is the same as understanding that you cannot *"heal"* someone else (because to heal is to love, and love is not an action). However, you can aid someone in their own healing by unconditionally loving them. Loving someone *as they are* naturally opens them to an inner state of self-acceptance where they can heal themselves by reconnecting an aspect of their love of self — an aspect that feels damaged through emotionally wounding experiences.

> *To believe you can "fix" or "save" someone*
> *is to try to use love as an action.*

Despite the intention, this comes from a place of judgment and control rather than from the empowerment of love. This is to explore conflicted qualities—*feelings that are being resisted*—which are projected out through a judgment of someone else as being *"in need of saving"* from those qualities.

None of us birthed in order *"to be saved by"* or *"to save"* anyone else (although we are free to explore those ideas as realities). If there is someone you want to help, then love them. This is not to love them *despite* what they are—*as in the "love the sinner, hate the sin"*—but to appreciate everything about them.

To love someone for who they are is to love them as they are now and in every moment. Through the allowance of unconditional love, it is realized that every self contains everything in existence. This is to know *self-as-all, self-as-unified,* and *all-are-one.* The understanding that *all are love* is the realization that everything has been created with love, which means everything can be met *within/through* the experience of love.

> *To love someone is to desire and act to make*
> *them more their self — not more your self.*

To love someone is to fuel and empower them — and not direct them. You are love. You are free. Free your love. To love is to free. *Recognize and know the power of your love by how it frees.* To know yourself as love is to know your freedom.

CLARIFICATIONS & REFLECTIONS

To judge someone is to believe that if you were stood in their shoes, you would have made a superior decision. To judge other people is to deny that we are each equal expressions of consciousness who birth from a state of reality where everything is known to be *connected/unified.* In just the same way that you will ultimately agree with your spirit's choice to birth *just as you are,* you will also agree—*when you embrace the perspective of your spirit*—with the choice of every other human being to birth just as they are. To know this interconnectedness and unity is to receive a sense of belonging in our shared human experience ... a shared journey of love.

> *Love is not a challenge to love the unlovable.*
>
> *Love is to see as your spirit sees.*

To unconditionally love someone who does not love themselves aids them in experiencing their conflicted qualities as undivided and lovable. This supports them in embracing themselves as being whole and perfect in their chosen imperfections. Unconditional love is infectious.

To awaken is to integrate with your spirit through the realization that separation is an illusion. This does not mean achieving some *'grand spiritual status'*; it simply, but profoundly, means discovering that *you are love.*

If the dream in your heart is to be a great spiritual master, know that this is no more and no less than being someone who loves *ALL* unconditionally. Feeling love in this way is to discover that not only are you love, but *ALL are love,* and *ALL are connected through that love.*

> *When you feel 'as one with all,' there is nothing but love for everything.*

Everything in existence can be met with love. Unconditional love is a state of joy and attraction to everything. It is a unifying force because it is felt equally for all things and qualities. By experiencing unconditional love, you become a potential point of unification between any two aspects of consciousness.

> *See how love bridges consciousness.*

Spirituality is not some complex mystery; it is about the realization and living of love. If your mind must name a goal, then let it be love.

> *You are love.*

> *All you need is love.*

> *Be love, and the reality you seek will be yours.*

PERFECTION THROUGH IMPERFECTION

*"I choose to experience the perfection
of my chosen imperfections."*

The realization of perfection lies within the liberation of what we have judged to be our imperfections. To become confident and fearless is not about being perfect. It is about accepting who you are right now — just as you are. To love yourself is to love *all that you are*, and in this love, you find the power to transform and grow.

You cannot love yourself by denying, minimizing, or tolerating what you consider to be your imperfections (as these are states of resistance). Only when you love and accept the qualities you have judged about yourself, such as your shyness, your impatience, or your self-doubt, will you see their gifts.

Learn to celebrate your imperfections
to see them clearly.

We are each our spirit in human form, and—*in alignment with our intention for this life*—we create every detail of that form. Regardless of whether you see a particular personal quality as positive or negative, you—*from the level of your spirit*—knowingly chose to experience yourself through it. These so-called imperfections shape our lives in powerful ways by causing us to engage with life through the characteristics that make us most different and unique.

Learning to appreciate your reasons for choosing your most challenging personal aspects is a part of accepting, surrendering to, and awakening the potential of your human self.

Your imperfections make you the ideal teacher of the lessons you have learned—*and are still learning*—through them. By standing in the freedom of this understanding, you can release your fears, unbind your mouth, and speak the dream that flows through your heart without reservation or attachment. To run from your imperfections is to run from yourself. To appreciate your idiosyncrasies—*as the gifts they are*—is to touch your spirit (because to love your imperfections is to appreciate the wisdom of your spirit's choice to be you). This is the freedom that flows from self-acceptance.

The intention of your birth was not to be everything or please anyone. You are here to be *YOU*, and that is to know—*without doubt*—that you are perfect in your chosen imperfections. You are a free expression of individuality from which your spirit looks out to see its own reflection through a human focus. To deny any aspect of your individuality is to deny how you chose

—*with infinite wisdom*—to experience yourself as a mortal embodiment of eternal consciousness.

Meet your perfection by knowing
your imperfection.

See your imperfection clearly by
realizing that it is perfection.

You are perfectly you and
you are perfect.

CLARIFICATIONS & REFLECTIONS

Your birth choice is your spirit's decision to create your human self. Before you were born, your spirit made a conscious decision about the kind of person you would be. Within this intention, what we call our imperfections are gifts of focus we have each sculpted for ourselves—*with love in the timelessness before our physical birth* —to shape our human experience.

Although your spirit determines your aspects and qualities, it does not predetermine the events you will experience in life (it only points to a general territory of experience). Your birth choice includes predetermined aspects such as your genetics and birth circumstances (such as the choice of your family, which is made with the full knowing of their mortal and spiritual intentions, characteristics, and probable paths in life).

Even after we accept that our human form is a choice, we still tend to resist what we are—*our birth choice*—through the idea that we could or should have made a better choice. This resistance changes as you awaken because, as you recognize and embrace the experience of your spirit, you will find you are simultaneously embracing your human self (and thereby your birth choice). To perceive from the level of your spirit is to step into the breadth of understanding from which it created the focus of consciousness that is *YOU*.

As you integrate your spirit, you will agree with all of its choices, including the decision to create you *exactly as you are*, including your so-called imperfections. This is inevitable because you are your spirit in mortal form. The separation between what you perceive as your spirit and your human self is the perceptual illusion on which the human experience of individuality is founded.

> *There is no separation between you*
> *and the choice to be you.*

Having confidence in yourself and being fearless in your self-expression is not about achieving some state of perfection. It is about accepting yourself *as you are* in each and every moment.

You will not find the freedom of self-confidence through tolerating or reluctantly not hiding what you see as your imperfections. These imperfections could be your shyness, your perceived physical flaws, or your past mistakes.

Discover how fearless you are by re-evaluating what you dislike about yourself so you can see the value those qualities bring to your life. Through this wider acceptance of *all that you are,* see how your greatest potential lies in what makes you unique (and not necessarily in the qualities society tells us to most value).

SHARE YOURSELF
FREELY

*"I choose to freely share myself with
the world through love."*

W hen you accept being alone in your path, you will no longer feel alone. And when you feel the courage to share your path with the world, the world will share its riches with you. Just as the only complete answer you hold is your own, the fulfillment of your intention for this life is also yours alone. This is to realize that —*even though your being represents a powerful answer*—you are not here to be anyone else's solution (as that is a state of dependency). Other people will certainly benefit from hearing your wisdom; however, understand that *the focus of your beliefs* is the answer to a question that is uniquely your own.

In sharing your personal answers you will be a stepping stone for others to discover their own truth, but you can never complete another person's journey for them (as no one can arrive at their own resolution if they only follow you).

To share your path is to be of
great aid to others.

Feel and express your beliefs in all their glory.Fully embrace your beliefs, even the ones that may be considered unconventional or unpopular. It means expressing them with confidence and passion, without fear of judgment or rejection.

Share your path and answers freely, knowing that life is infinite and bountiful and that there is enough for everyone to create the dream within their heart.

Share your truth without attachment to how others will receive it.

Share because your heart feels joy in sharing.

Share without the need for validation, and you will discover the deepest validation inside yourself. Share your truth without expecting others to agree. This is about expressing yourself authentically *without being attached* to how others will receive it. Anyone who purports to possess *"the one and only truth"* is not standing in their power.

Instead, they are caught in a struggle for external validation through an attachment to other people believing them (in order to feel safe believing it themselves). They fear being alone in their beliefs and, in their drama, may believe it is imperative for others to follow them in order to save humanity from itself or avert a disaster. Respect and love these people—*as to resist them is to further entrench their beliefs* —but do not buy into their drama unless their experience of reality is one you wish to experience for yourself.

Feel and believe in your own evolving truth.

Do not be reliant on others believing as you do in order to fully live in the way you feel to. Know you are capable of feeling something so strongly that you would *be willing to walk your path alone* in order to explore that feeling. Be clear in your personal truth, and do not be afraid to share it freely. You birthed into this world to feel and express *all that you are.*

CLARIFICATIONS & REFLECTIONS
While your spirit exists in a state of unconstrained freedom, your human self was birthed through an intention that expresses a strong degree of focus. You are not contained by the focus of this intention because the unconstrained experience of your spirit remains available while you are embodied. Although your intention for your life does not predefine its events, it does create the sense of direction and guidance you feel through the resonance of your heart.

> *The intention through which you birth can be felt across all levels of your being.*

Within your mind, it is felt as a question that seeks an answer. The journey that answering this question creates is best understood as a continual refinement of your mental understanding of the question (as opposed to the finding of a definitive answer). When you refine the understanding of your question, you will naturally evolve the definitions it is based on (which then shifts your relative position of belief within human definition).

For example, a part of answering the question *"Am I a good or bad person?"* is realizing that it is not an *'either-or'* question because there are ways in which ALL people reflect BOTH positive and negative qualities. The question continues to refine through evolutions such as *"What is it to see people as good or bad if all people are both?"* or *"Are the terms good and bad describing something real, or are they just a human construct?"* This process of refining the question is a journey of self-discovery, where your beliefs and perceptions evolve as you gain new insights and experiences.

These refinements of the question represent a continuing path of answering it, which then changes your experience of life in how it shifts the personal definitions—*and meanings*—through which you perceive reality.

Sharing yourself with others can be a source of joy, but this joy can be lost if you become attached to how your sharing is perceived. When you let go of control and release this attachment, it is remarkable how quickly you attract like-minded individuals. This form of sharing is exciting, liberating and unashamed, as opposed to being a calculated mental strategy aimed at creating a connection or a specific effect.

> *Connection comes from authenticity,*
> *not manipulation.*

In this reflection, see the difference between freely sharing yourself and the energy of wanting to affect people in a certain way — such as being liked. When you share yourself freely, you are not trying to impress or influence others. You are simply being *authentic/passionate* and true to yourself. Not only will other people best meet you when you share yourself freely, but this is how you will best meet the most joyful experience of yourself.

TRUTH IS PERSONAL
& EVOLVING

*"I choose to continually evolve and transform
my personal concept of truth, and thereby
my experience of self and reality."*

S piritual truth is personal, subjective, and constantly
changing. As you change your beliefs, so you shift
through realities — as you shift through realities, so
the expression of all truth shifts. To open yourself to the
realization that truth is not constant is to discover the power
to change your reality (as it is to allow the continual breaking
down and reinvention of your self-definition). In this state,
you are not only open to change, but you joyfully welcome it.

The allowance of your beliefs to change is your allowance of
your own evolution. You evolve as your beliefs do, and it is
you who evolves your beliefs. Hold no belief rigidly, and your

beliefs will move and evolve with you — allowing you to adapt to changing circumstances. Drop your resistance to life by being open to all possibilities. This allows your experience to flow.

Through rigidity, you only fight yourself.

It can be exciting to battle with your reflection by resisting your own experience, but if you are to engage in battle, do so with the awareness of your action as a creative choice. This is to be a conscious creator of your experience rather than someone who is unconsciously reacting to it.

Speak your truth clearly and without reservation, even if the beliefs you speak of today contradict what you said yesterday. Embrace such shifts in your truth as this is to fully embrace the potential for change within yourself. Do not allow yourself to be limited by a need to be consistent. Allow the impermanence of life to exist within your experience of self. Explore the freedom of changing your mind and know that if someone rejects you for changing your beliefs, they are simply at a point of wanting to move in a different direction.

When you change, rejoice!

Change is not something to be feared or resisted. Instead, it should be celebrated as a sign of your growth and evolution. Embrace change with joy and optimism, knowing that it is a vital part of your personal journey. It is a testament to your open-mindedness and adaptability, and a reminder that the only constant in life is change.

Trying to be consistent limits your ability to change and stifles the unfolding of your personal truth. We are each in a constant state of evolution through the integration of our experience. You cannot stop evolving because you cannot stop experiencing. While it is true that to integrate with your spirit is to remember *what you already are*, every moment of our spiritual journey evolves and directs our collective experience of being human.

> *Allow the knowing of yourself as a state of change to allow the space and movement necessary to realize that your freedom is eternal and your potential is infinite.*

CLARIFICATIONS & REFLECTIONS

While human, you are in a constant state of evolution through the integration of your experience. Your spirit does not evolve in the same outward way that you do in human form because it exists outside of the definition of time and space. However, it is not that your spirit is not evolving; we are our spirit in human form.

> *Our personal "human" experience of evolution is one face of our spirit's evolution.*

The choice to embody as you is the choice of eternal consciousness to experience a self that changes over time (which we call evolution). This is similar to saying that even though our spirit is immortal—*meaning it does not experience itself as mortal*—the experience of mortality is available through us. You are your spirit experiencing limitation, the finite, and evolution.

> *You are your spirit's experience of mortality.*

Compared to the breadth of awareness of our spirit, the human self is extremely limited in how it perceives; this does not make it inferior. Although much of our experience is expressed through limitation, we are infinite. For our finiteness to express our infinite nature, the human self—including our personal truth—is expressed as a state of change over time, rather than as fixed or absolute. This is one way our infinite spirit is expressed through our finite form.

It has been said that *"all suffering comes from seeking to become."* The state of *"not becoming"* points us to our spirit's frictionless, timeless, unchanging nature. To idealize this state over our human self is a denial of our spirit's choice to be human and exist within the change of linear time ... the experience of evolution. Our spirit and human self are not that different. Only their differing perceptual focus creates the illusion of there being a separation between them.

One effect of realizing that truth is subjective—*rather than fixed*—is that you will become more fluid and changing as a person. This release of rigidity—*a need for consistency*—comes through no longer fearing things changing. Although there is nothing wrong with enjoying consistency, recognize how you may be limiting yourself when that enjoyment of *consistency/comfort zones* becomes an attachment to things not changing.

Becoming aware of your resistance to change is an important tool in recognizing when fears are operating within you.

A NEW LEVEL OF CONSCIOUSNESS

"I choose to experience something new."

Within the relativity of the human experience, a new reality is birthing from within the old. The face of this new consciousness is birthing through the resolution of the past. The past is resolved through the realization of a new, wider perspective on what it means. The breadth of this perspective arises from remembering and integrating the wider state of existence from which we birthed the human experience. The integration of this ancient knowing into what we have become is creating a state of consciousness that bridges them both.

When you see the past anew—healing it
in the present—you are expanding what
consciousness knows itself to be.

The state of human consciousness that is birthing at this time has a face like no other. It is the face that knows not the past (for all is present), knows not suffering (for the perfection of all is seen), and knows not limitation (for even that which is felt to be limited is seen to be a choice made in freedom). The face of this new circle of consciousness is *birthing/revealing itself* through each one of us.

Each person has equal access to the newly imagined freedom of this realization of what it is to be human. Though it cannot be contained in definition, the many words that most point to this state of enlightenment are:

- *freedom, joy, and love.*

- *equality, respect, and cooperation.*

- *creatorship, clarity, and vision.*

- *sovereignty, fearlessness, and ease.*

The embracing of this new consciousness is the next step in our evolution. This new consciousness does not know truth as singular — it is *'All as Truth.'* It is a state of mind that embraces all perspectives and experiences as valid and true, leading to a profound sense of enlightenment and open-mindedness. This is the birth of the multi-perspective, where you experience life from the perspective *of the many*, as well as your own. This is the state of Unified Diversity; it is the face of the freedom we have sought.

> *This 'freedom consciousness' is changing everything.*

Only you have the power to make the choice to step into this new experience of reality. You are the architect of your own experience of self, and you can shape it into anything. If what you seek is joy and abundance, if what you seek is clarity in all things, then choose to shape the version of yourself that your heart yearns for.

You are the embodiment of all your choices. Choose to see the beauty in your own being to appreciate the beauty of your choices. Recognize the fresh excitement within the choice to start shaping the reality of your dream. This book was crafted to be a vessel and catalyst for that choice.

There is only one time — it is the Now.

Awaken and live your dream.

CLARIFICATIONS & REFLECTIONS

As you recognize linear time as an illusion and all experience as eternally present and available, there is a perspective from which it can be said that nothing is new. The term *'new'* only has relevance in the context of being new for the consciousness experiencing it.

For example, archaeologists make new discoveries by finding that which is old. Or, a geologist may crack open a geode and be the first person to see something a million years old. In just the same way, the new state of consciousness humanity is stepping into at this time is not something that did not exist before our experience of it; it is a new experience for our current state of consciousness (even when it has awoken to and integrated the unified, ancient consciousness which birthed the human experience). As such, the term *'new'*—*like any term with temporal implications*—is only meaningful when viewed from within a state of relativity (such as the linear time of the human experience).

The idea of *'new consciousness'* is not something unique to our time in history. It is not that the current awakening to newness has not happened before. The birth of humanity itself is the birth of new consciousness. The collective state of human consciousness has always been—*and will always be*—birthing new consciousness. The continual and consistent nature of this birth tends to make it unremarkable to us.

What makes the birth of this new experience of consciousness at this time in history particularly noteworthy—*such that some even call it a "great awakening"*—is that it describes the stepping out of our containment within polarized perception (a defining feature of the human experience).

Through this shift in perception, the new consciousness is a change in our fundamental nature and a shift in our primary experience of being human. Even though all change represents a shift from what we are into something new, it is the current shift from polarized perception that is being referred to when you hear of the *'new consciousness'* birthing at this time.

This is not only a spiritual awakening; it is being driven by seeing ourselves more clearly than ever through the many ways in which technology is exposing us to ourselves — without regard for our desire for censorship and secrecy.

TO PERCEIVE IS TO CREATE

*"I choose to experience my perception
as being a creative act."*

When embodied, we experience ourselves as contained within a moment of time and limited to a particular physical location. This experience of limitation and separation is a part of what forms the illusion of our individuality.

Despite this illusion, we constantly radiate our ideas, thoughts, and emotions across all of time and space. Our consciousness—*which is infinite*—is not limited by the containment of time, the crossing of distance, or the resistance of physical impenetrability.

*Each of us is a unique expression of the
infinite and eternal consciousness.*

Our spirit cannot be contained. Energy from our unified level of consciousness flows through each of us, connecting us beyond our current understanding. The eternal and timeless point of inspiration from which this book has birthed is common to all, and yet each of us will perceive and interpret it differently.

Perception is an act of creation.

Every realization you draw from this book is a contribution of your perspective to the creation of love in your hands. These words were written in *the Eternal Now*, and—*from the timeless perspective of our spirit*—it can be said that the writing on this page has been birthed from everyone who will ever read it. The words in front of you may have come from what appears to be an external source, but your experience of them is uniquely of your own creation.

Every person touched by an idea feeds the energy of that change back into its creation. Every person who finds meaning within these words has participated in the creation of these words. This then aids other people—*from across all of time and space*—in accessing their personally unique version of the realization.

You are present in the writing of these words because we are all one consciousness expressed as many intentions. We are each the composer of every experience we perceive. Deep within our collective heart, there is only one composer—*one unified state of consciousness*—that is infinitely expressed.

All realities flow through each other.

We continually perceive and radiate energy from across time and space. This blending of energies does not stop you from being you or me from being me. We are not the contents of a box. We are not any this or that. We are each an evolving expression of infinite consciousness expressed as a self.

CLARIFICATIONS & REFLECTIONS

Until you have felt the freedom of your spirit, it is hard to conceive of how time could be said to limit and separate us. To spirit, there is not an unalterable past or an unseeable future through which it can experience itself as separate from the events that form its experience. It cannot imagine the past and future as something it cannot directly perceive in *'the Now,'* and yet we each accept this separation from the events of our lives as *"just how it is."*

Spirit exists within a timeless state where *'timing'* is simply a marker point for an event — an event that is always available to be perceived (like a book in a library). In not experiencing the past and the future as a limit—*and how they separate us from the events of our life*—spirit has a radically different experience of time. Although this is generally described as *existing outside of time,* our spirit can also be thought of as *existing within the experience of ALL time.* In not being contained by the illusion of time, it can perceive across time. While we exist within the containment of time...

...our spirit knows time as a quality of existence it is free to traverse and perceive.

Because our spirit can—*whenever it chooses*—experience ANY time, it is said to exist in *the Eternal Now moment.* This is equivalent to being able to read every book in a library at once instead of one book at a time. You could imagine your spirit's infinite nature as stemming from its ability to choose each of your personal *'now moments'* from the infinity of ALL potential now moments. You then experience these moments in a linear sequence (which we call *"linear time")* instead of all together in *the Eternal Now* (which can be thought of as an infinite library of all possible events).

By learning to consciously connect with and feel your spirit, you will begin to feel humanity as a shared, collective level of consciousness. Everything you create and release into the world is only ever the seed of something that will continue to grow through the perception of other people. Everything evolves within linear time.

> *We are all here to create an experience not just as individuals, but as a collective.*

Within any shared event, do your best to appreciate what everyone brings to the table because you realize how each of our unique states of perception contributes to our collective experience.

MEETING
EVERYTHING

*"I choose to love myself through
loving the world."*

To share yourself with the world is to freely allow yourself to *be as you are*. For many, this is a journey of releasing shame and guilt and no longer identifying with feeling unworthy or undeserving. These aspects of fear each create their own unique fear of looking in the mirror of the world through the negative idea of being exposed to its judgment and condemnation. Inevitably, a part of releasing these fears is about facing your fear of the world—*and how it may treat you if you are transparent*—by allowing yourself to fearlessly be as you instinctively feel to be.

Because the world is a reflection, realize that this fear of how you may be treated stems from a belief that either you do not deserve to be treated well or that *'the world'* is a cruel place. Begin the transformation of these negative beliefs with the choice to treat yourself with love and respect. This is the choice to know and act from the basis that you deserve positive experiences — not because you have 'achieved worthiness,' but because you know that positive experiences reflect what you innately are.

Become clear and conscious of how you treat yourself to integrate that clarity of self-perception into your present-moment awareness that operates when you interact with the world.

> *When in freedom, there is no perception*
> *of a better or worse self.*

In freedom there is just the unfolding clarity of your experience of self. This clarity is the bigger picture by which you—*from the level of spirit*—are guiding your life. In this light, to identify your judgments is to gain clarity because to see them is to instantly begin their transformation.

Releasing judgment of yourself is a stepping stone to releasing judgment of the world. This is the journey of meeting yourself in the world and is to unify with the whole rather than judge or reject it. It is the release of the boundary of *isolation/separation* which has mentally evolved such potency in the human psyche.

> *Meet your fears to meet more of your self.*

Embrace your fears as a pathway to self-discovery. Each fear you meet is an opportunity to understand and accept more of yourself.

Meet more of your self to meet more of the world.

Meet more worlds to meet the universe.

Meet more universes to meet *the one unified consciousness.*

Meet the experience of *the one consciousness* to meet your self unfiltered.

There is nothing in existence that *the one consciousness* is not.

All that you fear will be experienced within the seeing of how it is that *you are everything.*

CLARIFICATIONS & REFLECTIONS
Fear of the world's reaction to you being yourself is the fear of being judged and condemned. This is, at some level, reflective of a fear of meeting your own judgment and condemnation. As long as you continue to judge yourself—*regardless of how loving you are towards others*—you will experience a reflection of that judgment of self.

Learning to not judge yourself is a journey through your fears, and it begins with ceasing to judge yourself for your own self-judgment. Scolding yourself for having negative thoughts will only ever reinforce—*and not release*—you from a feeling of negativity.

Accept that you have done nothing wrong
to feel this way about yourself.

Accept that your response to your life
has been perfectly understandable
and has not been lacking.

Release the cycle of self-judgment by practicing self-compassion. Your negative thoughts are not a reflection of your worth but a part of your journey towards self-acceptance.

Cease to judge your judgments to be released from their fear and associated beliefs in inequality and separation. When you know who and what you are, the judgments of others will have no power to cause you to perceive yourself negatively. If you doubt yourself, then see that the judgments of others are the gift of seeing the embodiment of that doubt, such that you can see, name, and release it.

Through understanding reality to be a mirror, begin the journey of accepting that your anger and frustration at the unconsciousness of this world is your own anger for what you perceive as your flaws (because even if you cannot see the world as a reflection of your present self, it is a reflection of the past selves you have been to become what you are now).

This is a difficult process as it is to become conscious of a level of denial through which you have sought to feel separate from the unconsciousness of this world. And, although you may have become conscious of many deep spiritual truths—*which remain unconscious to most people*—there are still many ways in which we all act unconsciously.

By recognizing your flavors of unconsciousness, you will gradually transform your negative reaction to the world's unconsciousness. Do not do this to try to be a more spiritual person — do it to free yourself from the negative effects you endure by seeing the world's unconsciousness through a lens of anger and frustration.

FLYING

"I choose to fly through life by releasing my attachments."

There are many wonderful experiences to be tasted in this world with which your heart may resonate. Enjoy these experiences, knowing them all as vessels full of potential for your own unfolding experience of life. There is no limitation to their bountifulness, and the more you allow yourself to flow into your experience—*without resisting it*—the more you will come to know yourself.

Allow yourself to flow with life.

Allow yourself to know you are the flow of life.

Enjoy the fruitful experiences of this world, but do not limit yourself by believing that your joy depends on maintaining any particular experience. There is no source of experience without which you would be diminished by anything other than your fear-based beliefs. Any feeling that says otherwise is a feeling of *attachment/dependence.* This is where you have given a part of the power of your consciousness to something you perceive to be external to you.

To be free of attachment is to realize there is no experience you cannot create for yourself. This is to know the blissful harmony—*rather than frustration and dissatisfaction*—that can exist between your desire for reality and your experience of reality.

The incredible flow within *consciousness/life* is the connection of all wanting and receiving. It is an ever-unfolding movement through ever-unfolding feelings of the fulfillment of self-exploration. It is the current of never-ending change that continually births from within all life.

Use this flow to throw off the shackles of limited thinking and fly into life through the knowing that you cannot be dependent on external things in a world you are creating. Know yourself as the creator of your experience to release yourself from the gravity of your fears. There is nothing that you lack. All experiences of lack are experiences of illusion you are choosing to create.

To know yourself as not lacking is to know yourself as free. This is to realize that you contain infinite potential through your ability to create your experience. Know this, and you will know your life as the feeling of effortlessly being in flight. Release the choice to be lacking, wounded, and attached … and you will feel the sky upon your feet.

You are creation in flight.

Know yourself as that which is flying.

CLARIFICATIONS & REFLECTIONS

Our sense of identity arises through joy and fear-based factors (expressed through what we do and don't like). We tend to see our attachments as being either positive or negative — usually with attachment to things considered positive being seen as good and attachment to things deemed negative being as bad. For example, attachment to alcohol is seen as bad, but attachment to your spouse or children is seen as good.

Another common way of perceiving this is through the idea that attachment through a feeling of love is positive, and attachment through a feeling of possessiveness is negative (so if your attachment causes you to become jealous and controlling, it is seen as bad).See how we typically experience attachments in a polarized way, where they are seen as either blessings or curses with no—*or few*—shades in between.

The reason for this polarization is that attachments carry an emotional charge because they represent a belief in a state of inequality, tension, and lack (rather than balance, harmony, and wholeness).

Attachment is fear-based.

Your attachments are relatively easy to identify and work with because—*although they are states of feeling*—they tend to be clearly (and sometimes dramatically) represented at the level of belief. For example, if you ask yourself questions about what would happen if you no longer had access to whatever you are attached to, you will quickly start revealing your limiting beliefs about that attachment.

To work with these beliefs, you can start by questioning their validity and imagining a life without the attachment. These beliefs will reveal the ways in which you believe you will be personally diminished by the loss of what you are attached to (which typically centers around the idea that your happiness, security, and well-being will be threatened). We believe that what we are attached to is somehow necessary or fundamental to what we are (meaning that without it, we are missing something vital we need to operate successfully). This belief reflects a lack of sovereignty, which is the knowing that you *are complete/have everything you need.*

To know yourself as a sovereign being is to be without attachment.

This is to feel as if you are flying because, without the weight of fear, that is what consciousness does.

TRUTH IS SUBJECTIVE

*"I choose to release the idea that
MY truth is THE TRUTH."*

There is no such thing as truth beyond the understanding of truth as the self-defining idea of itself. Even those who have seen through the illusion of an objective world still tend to hold on to the idea of an ultimate truth — an objectified level of realization believed to transcend all other knowing. This idea of *"The Truth"* is a concept that at one time served us in our exploration of individuality, but has now come to limit our idea of what we can be.

*This limitation is the result of following
of homogenized mental ideals rather
than the guidance of our feelings.*

On our spiritual journey, we often refer to ourselves as *'truth seekers'* — and rightly so. However, it is important to understand that *the truth we seek is uniquely ours,* as each of us possesses a distinct pattern of resonance. What we once may have considered *'The Truth'* is, in reality, only our personal truth in the present moment.

Truth is not some Holy Grail, and your version of the truth is no more valid or right than anyone else's. If you wish to think in such terms, call the Holy Grail *"fearlessly allowing yourself to be all that you feel to be."* This is to know you are free and the creator of your experience. Embrace this freedom in defining your truth, and feel the empowerment it brings.

> *Truth, like freedom, is not a state of ideas — it is a state of being.*

An idea can be a tool for freedom, but it is not freedom in and of itself. Ideas alone do not free people — people themselves choosing to live in freedom frees people.

> *Ideas/words can be a powerful catalyst for entering freer states of being, but they do not create freedom; they only ever point at the choice for it.*

Share your personal truth freely and with love, but understand that your ideas alone will not free people — yet they may use them to free themselves. In seeing this distinction, a spiritual seeker is freed from the search for an ultimate, idealized truth. This cannot exist as it would invalidate the freedom of our will to creatively perceive as we choose.

To stop the pursuit of *'The Truth'* is to find what you've been searching for — the understanding that *truth is what you shape it to be.* This is the realization that your human experience is a *result/manifestation* of your chosen beliefs. Embrace the evolving nature of truth, and feel the openness and adaptability it brings to your understanding.

Do not objectify or worship truth.

You are more than your truth — you are a state of being. Truth is no more and no less than what you decide it to be and that our choices are only ever in the moment and for that moment.

Cherish truth as you cherish yourself
— as a constantly evolving, beautiful
manifestation of eternal consciousness.

CLARIFICATIONS & REFLECTIONS

Our embodied ability to be unconscious and forget creates our experience of true and false. To believe in *"The Truth"* is to believe in an ultimate, transcendent state of definition that is always correct. But consciousness—*not definition*—is the basis of reality. What we call *"truth"* is a human construct that—*from the perspective of our spirit*—is only understood in relation to other definitions of truth.

When we believe *"I have discovered THE TRUTH!"* we feel powerful and in control. The potency of this feeling arises from the personal liberation we experience when self-identifying with our sense of truth. However, this carries the limited notion that there is an evolutionary end-destination. This idea is unimaginable to our spirit as—*being eternal*—it knows there is no end to experience (as there are an infinite number of potential experiences of realizing *"The Truth"*). The entrenched concept of *"The Truth"* (which allows for powerful emotions such as righteousness and judgment) can only exist through the denial of—*or resistance to*—that which opposes it.

Only within the polarization of our individuality is there the potential of perceiving something as being false (or without value).

"NOT true" is meaningless to our spirit because—*in being infinitely free*—it is free to experience any statement as truth. To call something *"false"* is only to state—*from your embodied perspective*—how you want to perceive it. For example, you can state that you are mortal—*and call it a self-evident truth*—but your spirit knows your potential to live within the embodied state for as long as it likes. It sees your statement of *"I am mortal"* not as the truth (or *'not truth'*) of how reality eternally is, but as your personal choice of perspective in the moment (with there being no concept of true or false about it).

All definitions exist in relation to each other because statements of truth are only ever personal and of the moment (meaning they are impermanent and subjective because they are experienced through individuality). Your perception of definition changes in relation to your ever-evolving self-definition as well as in relation to your consciousness (versus unconsciousness) of *ALL* possible definitions.

ALL definitions contain powerful truths when viewed from certain perspectives (and falsehoods when viewed from others).

NO THING SEPARATES
YOU FROM JOY

*"I choose to live by using my feeling of
joy as my primary guidance."*

No single outward *'thing'* is necessary for joy. You
are engaging your path if you are feeling either joy
or fear. Understanding how you are on your path is
not required to experience the joy of your path. In life, there
is the constant choice of joy or fear. To manifest the choice for
joy is to decide—*with all your being*—that you are ready for and
deserve to feel joy.

*Everything before you on the plate of
your life is there for a reason.*

Do not doubt this — to do so is to live in a reality where you
believe mistakes exist. There are no mistakes. If there is a
persistent morsel of food on the plate of your life that you do

not like, eat it to find out why it is there, and you will move beyond it. In this way, you will make room for something new.

There is nothing more important or more spiritual than being in your joy.

There is no spiritual truth, ideal, or goal that requires you to sacrifice your joy. The pursuit of spirituality and joy, when viewed from the heart, are one and the same. To enter your joy, you must transform your feelings of shame and guilt and release self-limiting beliefs. Your desires are not dangerous temptations — they are the compass guiding you to your joy.

It is time to transform any feelings that you still have around the need for salvation, redemption, or forgiveness. No one died for your sins because there were no sins to die for. In relation to Christian terminology, *'The Cross'* symbolizes the shame and guilt that humanity still carries and is something that each person touched by that religion must put down of their own accord. To see Christ on the Cross (or any other religious equivalent) is to see yourself as deserving of—*or desiring of—* crucifixion or martyrdom.

Do not do anything from the idea of it being for a *'higher purpose.'* Do it because you feel to. Do it because you want to. Then, and only then, will you be radiating the fulfillment of your intention for this life. Only then will you be living the legacy spoken of by the great spiritual masters (such as Jesus Christ, Buddha, Sri Krishna, Jane Roberts, and Lao-Tzu). If the salvation of religion exists, then it is the realization of joy and not death. You do not need to die. You do not need to be *'saved.'*

You need to live.

Live in joy.

CLARIFICATIONS & REFLECTIONS

Your *'path'* refers to the ongoing fulfillment of the feeling-based intention that created your mortal life. This is a path without a strict definition or destination because there is no end to the ways in which you can fulfill your *path/intention* for this life.

Whether or not you currently identify as religious, the human belief in mistakes was founded in religion and its idea of original sin. This is the belief that because we experience pain and suffering in human form, we must have committed some mistake or crime for which we are being punished until we redeem ourselves.

> *When the guidance of your feelings is followed—rather than the mental judgment and division of good versus bad—you will discover that all that arises through the following of your heart is valuable.*

And when that value is felt, no experience can be seen as a mistake. The fear-based idea that it was a mistake to create a reality that is not based solely on joy has been a defining part of what it is to be human (one that religion embodied and then fostered through its teachings around sin, guilt, and shame).

The idea of correcting a mistake or sin is the feeling behind the concept of *'the greater good.'* This is where logical, mental arguments are used to justify doing something that feels antagonistic to how we feel as a person (*"We must kill them, or they will kill us"*). This is not about mental arguments being used to justify something that is *'morally wrong'*; it is internal logic being used to justify actions we do not feel good about (having concluded that we do not have a choice).

This is a clear example of the subjugation of feeling by thought and is the basis of what allows the human experience to be so polarized. This is because it is governed by our mental fears alongside the unifying love of all that innately emerges from following our *hearts/inner guidance.*

Our mind is an incredible creation that makes the human experience possible by opening us to unexpected and diverse possibilities. Approach the exploration of this diversity through the understanding that the basis of life is joy.

The more you embrace diversity, both internally and externally, the more you meet and recognize the beauty of what is shared.

By using your feelings as your primary guidance—*which is to embrace allowance and inclusivity*—you can find peace in any moment. Listen to your feelings and let them guide your choices. When you do this, you will find that your actions are in harmony with your dream for this life giving you a stable, reliable sense of peace and fulfillment.

YOU ARE WORTHY
OF YOUR DREAM

"I choose to take the conscious awareness and appreciation of my worth into all situations."

To allow your dream will take but one thing: deeming yourself worthy of it. Throughout our lives, we are told repeatedly, and in many ways, that we are not worthy of our dream. That undermining statement—*regardless of its source*—is a lie that separates us from the knowing of our spirit.

Are you willing to allow yourself the realization that you are absolutely and uniquely special?

Are you willing to proactively live your dream instead of just hoping for it?

Are you willing to give yourself what you want?

Are you ready to admit to yourself exactly what you 'really' want?

Whatever your dream is, realize that to live it, you must first accept it as your dream. Feel the ways in which you resist the acceptance of your dream. Feel the ways in which you have judged your dream.

Accept your dream to accept yourself.

All you value in others, but not yourself, is an aspect of your worth that you have externalized. Part of fully discovering your incredible value is drawing back into yourself the power you have given away. To believe you still need to prove your worth is to believe that your worth lies in some act ... an act you deem you must perform in order to be worthy.

*Worthiness is a feeling,
not an action.*

To allow the feeling of worthiness and being deserving into yourself is but a choice, and that is the choice to see yourself through eyes of love and acceptance. To know, feel, and determine your worth is to put down the emotional baggage you have accumulated.

If you believe any other person has damaged your feeling of self-worth, then know you have the power to take that worth back. See whatever they said or did as the fear-based distortion it is. Realize how you gave your power away by believing in that *distortion/lie/manipulation/disguise* (because of how it reflected fears within you).

*The dream in your heart is there for only
one reason — for you to live it.*

It is possible to live the dream in your heart. To do so, you must step out of your own way. The only thing that separates you from your dream is the belief that it is not possible. Know, with a unity of heart and mind, that your dream is possible, and you will instantaneously start to experience its unfolding.

Allow this knowing to be your knowing.

Allow yourself the experience of your dream unfolding.

You are worthy and always have been.

You are a valuable being.

*The best time to feel your worth is—
and will always be—NOW.*

CLARIFICATIONS & REFLECTIONS

The dream that flows through your heart arises from the meeting of your intention, the human experience, and the limitless imagination of your spirit. Being a feeling-based intention, your dream does not birth from any specific *'this'* or *'that'* but from the desire for the overall feeling of an experience. We may, for example, dream of being an effective leader, but without defining a specific leadership position within the world. Our dreams are fluid and adaptable to any circumstance.

The imagination is best thought of as being *'of the heart'*—*rather than the mind*—due to its instinctive, non-linear nature. It represents your access to the infinite potential to change because to become something, you must first imagine it. The imagination is your greatest resource because it is the part of you least limited by your beliefs (because its nature is part of the human experience that cannot be quantified).

The fusion of your heart and imagination is where you retain the potential for the most intimate experience with your immortal, non-physical nature (your spirit). It is the place where these *words on paper* are emerging into this physical reality through the direction of perception within consciousness.

These words are not *'The Word of God'* in religious terms; they are the embodiment of feeling expressed into definition. As such, they are what we each are — God within a state of human definition. Your words are the *Word of God,* and your touch is the *Touch of God.*

A part of becoming a conscious creator is seeing that it is the way you feel about yourself—*and not how anyone else or society feels about you*—that ultimately determines the level of worth you are willing to assign to yourself. As a conscious creator, you have the power to shape your reality through your thoughts, feelings, and actions. Feeling badly about yourself is to consistently feel bad, and that masks the positive feelings of guidance through which you can most joyfully navigate the human experience. You will not find what you seek as long as you punish or berate yourself.

Only through loving yourself
will you find freedom.

REALIZING UNITY
WITHIN DIVERSITY

*"I choose to unify by celebrating
diversity rather than ideals."*

D o not fear that you are alone in your state of being, for you are not. Face your fears to meet your spirit. Through awakening to your spirit, you will discover that you are within a world of spiritual beings, each with an intention for this life that is equally as grand and special as your own.

*Live the dream that flows through your
heart; it is a description of your joy.*

This is to experience the kind of bliss religion purports to await *'some of us'* in the afterlife. What religion calls *'Heaven'* is a state of being that exists within you in *the Now moment*. It is a state of consciousness that calls to you to be realized *in this lifetime* and not in some distant future we are disconnected from until death. You will return to what you perceive as a blissful state when you die, but that bliss is available to you now.

Your dream is a realization—*through feeling*—of what the potential of your reality can be. To truly realize something is to birth it into being; it is not to merely understand it intellectually. To realize something is to *BE* it.

> *Realization is not a mental state — it is the bringing into being of your spirit.*

To fully know something is to realize, feel, and experience it with *all your being.* Allow yourself to feel what you experience with *all your being,* and you will feel the reality of *all that you are* — and that is *God/the Creator/the one consciousness/the one self.* This deep introspection will connect you to the reality of your being.

> *Realize, know, and BE all that you are.*

This is to know that you are infinite and not doubt that realization. To be within this state of freedom is to *BE* your spirit within your embodiment, and that is the creation of *bliss/'Heaven'* on Earth.

The realization of our infinite potential, which all awakening individuals seek, can only arise from the realization of connection within. This is the meeting of *the one consciousness/the infinite* within you, and with that revelation comes the realization that *all are one.* This is the path back to unity from within division, and it is the path of seeing through the illusion of separation (which is seeing through the illusion of your fears). It is *the one consciousness* realizing into being the connected state of Unified Diversity, a state where we are all unique individuals, yet we are all connected and part of a larger whole.

The unification of humanity will celebrate —not repress—its diversity; the knowing of connection cannot be realized any other way.

Without an acceptance of all, there is not a complete acceptance of anything. Unified Diversity is the evolution of the *separate-contained-self* into *all-as-connected*. It is the realization of unity arising from a realization of equality within the self.

CLARIFICATIONS & REFLECTIONS

To awaken to *all that you are* from within human form is to enter a state of Unified Diversity. Awakening, in this context, refers to a spiritual realization of our interconnectedness be seeing through the illusion of separation.

Typically, we do not awaken to the illusion of our human individuality until physical death. Through spiritual awakening, you can see through the illusion of separation while still embodied. This creates a state of consciousness where you know yourself as unified with all life, and yet, you are still within the perception and appreciation of difference and individuality. This is the state of Unified Diversity, which possesses the qualities of both spirit and the human self in an integrated state.

A Unified Diversity can be thought of as a collective of individuals in a state of directly perceiving how they are connected. As such, it is a relatively shallow level of individuality compared to someone who experiences feeling disconnected because they are different (a common quality felt within the human experience).

To feel both diverse and unified, individual and collective, *'as one'* but *'with many,'* is one way in which bliss can be consistently experienced from within embodiment. Because of this, it is easy to believe it is *'the ideal'* state of consciousness. However, a person who views the state of Unified Diversity as an ideal that can be achieved will not be able to meet it inside of themselves because—*by seeing it as a superior state*—they denigrate their own experience (and thereby exclude themselve).

An ideal is a hierarchical, human, mental construct, and, in relation to spiritual awakening, there is often an idea that the purpose of this *'inferior'* human life is to awaken into the *'superior'* state of Unified Diversity. Viewing the state of Unified Diversity as an ideal leads to a sense of inferiority, as it implies that our current state is not good enough. As the state of Unified Diversity is within the knowing of *the equality of all,* it cannot be fully met by any state of individuality that holds a superior, separatist belief about itself.

> *Unified diversity and consciousness of equality are two sides of the same coin.*

Ideals can never resolve the fractious aspects of the human condition. Humanity cannot be perfected into a homogenized ideal. In loving *all that we are,* so we must love *all we have been.* The state of Unified Diversity is a state of inclusion rather than *refinement/perfecting/idealization* through the exclusion of what is judged to be imperfect. It describes the state of unconditional love where all are loved equally (including yourself).

LIVE YOUR DREAM

*"I choose to share the dream that
flows through my heart."*

Y ou are uniquely special. The paradox (the circular
question and answer) that you contain is uniquely
yours. The path to its resolution is the living of the
dream in your heart. To fully know your dream, you must first
open your heart. To fully open your heart is to love yourself
without reservation.

To unconditionally love yourself, you must love *all that you
are.* There is a paradoxical circularity here as you must love
your flaws—*not commonly seen as beautiful*—to fully see your
beauty. The appreciation of your own beauty is a part of
valuing yourself. This is necessary to embrace and live your
dream. Honor your feelings by being the self they lead you to.

*To love and accept your human self is to deem
yourself worthy of experiencing your spirit.*

There is a *God/an All That Is/a Tao/a state of unified consciousness,* and it is the source of all beings (which is to say all realities). There is one consciousness, and you are it experiencing itself in a state of limitation. So, from that perspective, you are more limited than it, but you cannot be less than it because you are it—*the one consciousness*—choosing to be in a state of perceived limitation.

You chose to live this human life with infinite wisdom and clear intention. Within the realization of that intention lies your joy because the fulfillment of that intention is joy.

> *The expression of joy is the expression of love.*

> *The expression of love is the acceptance of the moment.*

> *The acceptance of the moment is the acceptance of the self.*

To deeply understand anything is courageous and shows your willingness to expand. Beyond understanding is the joy of being. Beyond realizing the shape of your dream is taking the step—*both inwardly and outwardly*—to live that dream. If you only keep your dream within the reality within your mind, then that is the only place it will exist.

There is no facet of your mind that you cannot express out into reality and live through the vitality of the human experience. You only need to believe that you can. Start by verbalizing your dream.

> *Words are a spell.*

When you speak them, so you create. Speak your dream, and you will begin its manifestation. Begin to walk that path with confidence, and you will be in joy. Joy is the realization of your dream, from the moment when you first conceive of it ... to the moment when you are living it.

Joy is not for the future.

Joy is for now.

CLARIFICATIONS & REFLECTIONS

The human mind thinks in a linear way because our mental processes have formed around the linearity of our language. This makes us want the answers to questions to be *one way or the other/true or false.*

The resolution to paradox is to see how paradoxical questions can possess opposing answers. For example, *'Is the Earth light or dark?'* Answer: sometimes, it reflects the light of daytime and sometimes the dark of nighttime. Neither answer is wholly correct; both answers are discovered to have a circular relationship. The answers to most spiritual questions take this form and lead to the realization that...

*...all answers contain value and
truth from a perspective.*

Answers that seek to be *'definitive'* are exclusionary by nature. Answers that seek levels of truth drawn from all perspectives are inclusive by nature. This inclusivity is what connects us all, making us part of a larger whole. To be a defined individual is necessarily based on exclusion. However, once within the containment of individuality, you do not have to maintain an exclusionary standpoint in order to remain embodied.

Once embodied, being exclusionary will increase your depth of individuality through separation and is likely to be embodied in such feelings as righteousness, disconnection, alienation, superiority, inferiority, and competition. Being inclusive will lessen the sensation of individuality and is embodied in feelings of love, unity, connection, support, and cooperation.

As eternal consciousness, we created the human experience to explore *BOTH* directions (inclusive and exclusive). To be engaging with these words, you are currently engaging the collective choice to awaken (which includes breaking down the mechanisms of exclusion at a mass level). You are a part of both an individual and a mass choice to awaken to the illusion of separation.

> *The diffusion of our fears is an act*
> *of becoming more inclusive.*

But remember, no ideals ... you are not here to be inclusive or exclusive, cruel or kind, good or bad. You are not here to be any particular thing ... any particular *'this'* or *'that.'*

> *You are here to follow your heart*
> *wherever it leads you.*

YOU ARE NOT YOUR PAST

*"I choose to experience myself as who I
am in the present rather than through the
idea of who I am based on my past."*

T he potential of your dream exists in every moment.
Your past is something with which you can either
empower or disempower yourself. Do not be afraid of
the idea that in each moment, you are just beginning, for in
this understanding lies a great freedom. The universe was not
created billions of years ago; it is being created right now, and
you have the freedom to shape it as you wish.

*In each moment, the universe is created anew. This is to
realize that you are free and not constrained by what
came before.*

*In each moment, there is the potential for everything to
change*

*In each moment, that potential is fulfilled, and
everything changes.*

In each moment, you recreate the universe in new and exciting ways.

It is not the past that determines your present — it is you. Your choices, your actions, and your perceptions have the power to shape your present.

The degree to which your present moment comes to reflect and adhere to your past is purely a representation of the level of belief you are carrying that your past dictates your present and future. It is a common rut to perpetually recreate the pain of your past by holding a belief in its power over you and focusing on it.

> *Until you stop the pain in your past*
> *from creating fear for your future, you*
> *will be stuck in a loop of reliving it.*

To break the repetition of this cycle, you must take your power back from the pain. Do this by allowing yourself to completely feel it. Allow it to make you stronger by taking back your power from it.

If you choose to carry pain from your past, then realize that, on some level, you must believe that you need it. You do not need this pain. You do not need *any* pain. You no longer need its limits.

Just because your past was one way does not mean your future will be the same (unless you resign yourself to that belief). Do not get lost in the pain written in your story. Take back your power from your past.

> *Your self-doubt is powerfully reflected in*
> *your reality; only you have the power to*
> *go out and prove your doubts wrong.*

You are not your past.

However, if you mentally and emotionally live in your past, you will continually recreate it in your present moment. If you are mentally stuck dwelling in the past, open yourself back up to it so you can fully feel, experience, and release it. All things cease to perpetuate once fully experienced because they no longer hold any message for you.

Empower yourself by consciously evolving
an empowered perception of your past.

This could involve reframing past experiences in a positive light, acknowledging the lessons learned, and using them as stepping stones for personal growth.

CLARIFICATIONS & REFLECTIONS
In addition to the traditional, outward meanings of past and future, there is the way in which they each exist within us as a feeling-based idea that we have a relationship with. To become conscious of the story of our past and the belief in what our future will be is to acknowledge what powerful symbols our expectations and regrets have become.

You have the power over how you choose to perceive and express these symbols, as well as the way in which you allow them to shape the choices you make in your experience of the present moment. To be conscious of this choice is to have an empowered relationship with the quality of time. This is to discover that linear time is not inherently limiting. Do not experience yourself as a victim in relation to time through feelings such as regret and anxiety or by carrying stressful beliefs in the jeopardy of running out of time.

Once you are empowered in your feelings
for your past and future, you will also
be within an empowered relationship
with the passing of time.

In this state, with your past and future not being used as symbols of disempowerment, you will find that the idea of your past and future becomes less and less relevant. When you allow your complete self to be expressed into the present moment, your past and future are no longer necessary as extensions to your vessel of self. This is to step into ever-shallower experiences of linear time, just as you are stepping into ever-shallower experiences of individuality and are moving closer to the experience of your spirit (which is not contained within linear time) ... a state where the past and future lose their hold on you, and you can fully immerse yourself in the present moment.

'How you feel about your past' is the feeling
with which 'you create your future.'

Open yourself to recognize any pain from your past that still exists within you. The process of re-orienting yourself to exit this painful rut is one of choosing to *'become conscious of your mental focus'* such that you maintain a positive focus on creating in the present rather than a regretful focus created by repetitive thoughts about your past.

THE EFFORTLESS
TRANSFORMATION OF FEAR

*"I choose to move towards my fears such
that I transform them and release their
gifts of empowerment into my life."*

You are not living in freedom when you resist the unfolding of your experience. The greatest fears come from the fear of realizing your dream into reality. Between you and the realization of your dream is nothing but the illusion of your fears.

Confronting your fears is not a path of harm but of empowerment. Face your fears with a loving heart and an open mind, and watch as your they have no choice but to transform. Each fear is a reflection of the power you have given away. When you face a fear, you reclaim that power, bringing you closer to the conscious realization and integration of your spirit.

Fear of your dream is based on the idea that you are not worthy of it — not good, worthy, or deserving enough. The way out of fear is to realize that if you embrace your fears —*rather than resist them*—they will act as signposts to your dream. This is to understand that we are the ones who created our fears to hide our spirit from our human selves. Becoming conscious of your fear is the clearest path to lead you back to your dream.

> *Your fears are a trail of resistance that*
> *will lead you to the part of yourself that*
> *does not know fear (your spirit).*

Rejoice in the discovery of a new fear, for it signals that you are on the brink of transformation. With each release of resistance, you will experience a growing sense of freedom.

> *Every fear, when undone, becomes*
> *a stepping stone to freedom.*

This journey is not about pain but about joy and optimism as you watch your fears transform into opportunities for growth and empowerment, leaving you uplifted and inspired.

Experiences of being *"not free"* arise from the fear of freedom. Your freedom is always what you are ultimately moving toward when facing your fears. Some fears are so old that they only exist in the mind and can be let go through no more than the acknowledgment they exist.

Letting go of fear does not need to be painful, but sometimes you will insist on pain because you want to feel you have worked hard to overcome your fear (a belief in the necessity of effort). Sometimes, you will subconsciously ask for a fear-releasing experience to be difficult—*or even painful*—in order to not judge yourself for carrying the fear for as long as you have, as well as to help you believe it has *'really'* been released.

> *Fears can be dissolved with nothing*
> *more than your conscious intent and*
> *resolve to integrate them.*

There is no need to struggle with your fears — simply turn your attention to them and watch as they disperse in the clarity of awareness emanating from your heart ... watch them dissolve through the power of your conscious intent.

CLARIFICATIONS & REFLECTIONS

Fear can be seen as a repulsive force in an attractive universe. It allows us to put our consciousness of connection into our unconsciousness by creating a fear-based meaning. In doing this, we end the experience of being fully unified with our source—*the one consciousness*—and instead experience ourselves as individuals. This is the mechanism by which fear shapes our perception of reality and our sense of self.

> *Choosing to experience fear is a process of*
> *suppressing information about what you*
> *wish to fear, such that you experience at*
> *least one quality of it as unknown.*

A fear-based idea is then creatively projected onto this unconsciousness, such that a negative, prejudiced meaning is attached. The internal negative charge within this meaning is then experienced through the quality of external separation. Recognizing this process helps us understand how fear is created and maintained in our consciousness. The creation of fear is both meaningful and purposeful in how it has expanded our experience of individuality.

By realizing your fears are an illusion you have created to form your individuality, recognize that your fears are based on your negative feelings (rather than clear observation). As such, instead of treating your fears as *'lessons learned'* that protect you from harm—*through a belief in their validity*—choose to view them as your self-chosen, self-limiting beliefs. Be open to seeing that what you fear—*as with all things in life*—is a reflection of a part of yourself that you are currently resisting.

As satisfying as it is to transform fear in this way, remain conscious that the primary flow of energy in your life comes from the passion you feel in your heart. Through the transformation of your fears, your passion will start to feel ever stronger. This empowerment, derived from the catalytic flow of this joy-based feeling, allows you to effortlessly transform your fears. This allows you to remain focused on your unfolding passion rather than the resolution of your fears.

Through this practice, you will not become self-identified with the transformation of fears more than the following of your heart (and yet, through the following of your heart, you are sometimes led to transform your fears).

JOY AS THE INFINITE SELF

*"I choose to radiate the joy I feel
flowing through my heart."*

Embracing the feeling of joy is not just a state of being; it is a transformative force. It is the path to realizing your dreams — a journey of unfolding joy. Follow this feeling of joy; it is the essence of your limitless self — a state of freedom consciousness.

Joy is not just a feeling; it is a connection. It is the sensing, the touching of your spirit, and it is what unites us all in a shared experience of life.

Joy is that which your heart most wants. *Joy is the feeling you have assigned to everything you seek.* To seek your dream is to seek your joy. The route to freedom is not a path of redemption, purity, righteousness, or sacrifice. It does not require giving up what you want and living in modest subservience. Freedom does not lie in ritual or penance, and it is not found in seeking some eternal deity's forgiveness.

The only forgiveness you need is your own.

The act of self-forgiveness is liberating, freeing you from the burden of guilt and allowing you to move forward with a sense of peace and acceptance.

The route to what religion calls *"salvation"* is through the allowance—*rather than denial*—of all your heart desires. This is *'salvation'* from your fear. No one dreams of suffering, being caged, or becoming trapped in a belief in lack. The realization of all dreams comes through the knowing that the self is unlimited, infinite, and free.

All limitations are self-manifested
illusions created by your fear
of being all that you are.

Because you see suffering in the world around you, do not fear that there is something selfish in seeking your joy. The ending of mass suffering comes from each individual choosing to live through the passion and guidance of their heart.

When living in joy, you will radiate that joy and, in doing so, aid others in finding their own. Joy will connect you with the world and everything in it. It will make you more compassionate, not less. The attainment of your joy is not some perk of reality. It is your responsibility to yourself if you wish to experience and share the magnificent potential of your spirit and its ever-unfolding path of joy.

All states of being are naturally infectious.

Whether you interact with them or not, what you feel touches the people around you. You are a beacon of your being. Radiate joy. Smile at strangers, express gratitude, and share your positive energy. Radiate love. Show compassion and understanding. Radiate *all that you are*. Instill the world with your happiness, and you will transform it far more than if you radiate pity, sorrow, or anguish for the suffering of others.

CLARIFICATIONS & REFLECTIONS

Freedom Consciousness refers to the state of existence that spirit exists within. In relation to the human experience, it is best understood as the freedom of consciousness experienced when you are not in a relationship with a repulsive or resistant force (such as fear). It is also commonly referred to as the state of *'Enlightenment'* or, in religious terminology, *'Christ Consciousness,'* which is a state of being fully aware of and connected to the infinite.

In terms of human perception, *'freedom consciousness'* refers to unpolarized perception. In polarized perception, what is perceived is compared against a scale (polarity) through which it is judged to be more one way than another (e.g., short as opposed to tall). Through this, things are perceived to be different to the point of being separate from all that is not like them.

In unpolarized perception, what is perceived is seen as being like an individual facet of a single diamond. The difference between things is still perceived, but there is no charged, polarized scale through which to perceive that difference as a state of separation. Everything is always seen to be *connected/ unified* at its root.

In our deepest heart, we are all one.

Unpolarized perception is the natural state of all beings that have not entered into a state of unconsciousness/ individuality.

Through our elevation of rational thinking, we have come to see emotions as states of feeling that—*despite arising in response to our experience*—are not seen to contain any additional information about that experience. Just as my fears are purposeful and meaningful, so are my joys. Through the fusion of clear thinking and recognizing that your emotions are giving you valuable information, bring the advantages of both perspectives together.

> *Your heart and mind do not need to*
> *be experienced as separate.*

The feeling of joy within you is the feeling of your spirit within your human form. By sharing this joy with others, you will be sharing the gift of yourself with this world, and you will live not only in a more joyous reality but also within the meeting space where we can best experience the potential of the power of our cooperation.

BE HAPPY FOR OTHERS

*"I choose to celebrate the presence
of joy within all."*

To love *where you find yourself* is to love yourself, even though it appears external. Free yourself from the idea that the grass is always greener somewhere else. This kind of divisive belief continually drains your power, hindering you from fully realizing the wonders of your spirit.

To always see reality as being better elsewhere is to wish to be someone other than who and what you are. It is to believe that *what you are* is inferior to *what you could be*. And that is to denigrate your current manifestation of self.

*To love where you are, wherever that
may be, you must love yourself.*

This archetypical energy of wanting what you do not have or wanting to be where you are not is the manifestation of *a belief in lack.* If you put energy into this belief, reality will always validate it by showing you that love and joy are everywhere except where you stand.

Allow yourself to want.

Allow yourself to want more.

Do this from a feeling of joy and appreciation for what you want. It does not need to come from a point of disrespecting or diminishing what you have. By following your feeling of joy, you will manifest your heart's desire. You can accept and love what you have and still want more. Do this by living in the acceptance of yourself as you are rather than from a focus on what is yet to come.

Through this understanding of *'loving the self that is present,'* learn the power of being happy for others *where they are* without it causing you to no longer want to be *where you are.* This does not mean that others no longer inspire you, but if perceiving another person does change you, then it is from a point of being inspired to be more rather than from seeing yourself as being less.

To envy others is only to harm yourself, as the joy of others will become a pain that surrounds you and disconnects you. To see joy in another and be angry that it is not your joy is the choice to live with anger as your companion, rather than joy.

The choice for joy is always present.

The present *'Now'* moment is the point of *choice/power.* When you are truly happy for others, you will share in their happiness in ways you did not realize were possible. To be envious of another is to separate yourself from your own happiness.

To be happy when good things happen to
others is to share in their happiness.

CLARIFICATIONS & REFLECTIONS
We often see in others the qualities we resist or deny in ourselves. This *'projection of self'* happens because we do not want to acknowledge those qualities within ourselves. However, since we live in a world that reflects who we are...

...what we refuse to see in
ourselves we see in others.

The choice to not see something in yourself is the choice to see it in another — this is a defining human *quality/limit/gift.* This reflection in another person is done through some form of negative judgment because the basis of the projection is *a fear-based resistance to a quality of self.* When you consciously choose joy over fear, you liberate yourself from this cycle of projection, taking control of your own happiness and growth.

The belief that "the grass is
always greener" somewhere else
is a form of projection.

This projection has the same essence of *not wanting to look at a quality as being within yourself* and instead focusing on finding a solution to what you are feeling somewhere outside of yourself. The profundity of the teaching that what you seek is already within you (popularized in L. Frank Baum's *The Wizard of Oz*) is easily missed because we tend to think that our intellectual understanding of it as a principle is enough. Comprehending the human tendency to project does not stop a person from unconsciously engaging in it.

Learn to sense when you are projecting
your fear/own qualities onto others.

To not be surrounded by unconscious projections of your fears come when your understanding of projection starts to act at the instinctive level — specifically at the level of awareness that you quickly realize when your focus ceases to be joy-based. This is to become conscious of when you are focused on *'what other people need to do'* instead of being focused on yourself (as this reflects when you are within the idea that what you seek is not within your grasp alone).

The projection of fear is revealed when you
find yourself focusing on what others should
do rather than on your own growth and joy.

On the spiritual path, it is important to distinguish between what your heart desires, which is infinite and fearless, and what your wounded mind thinks it needs to feel better. Understanding this difference will transform your reality and empower you to further unfold your heart.

Within each moment, there is the choice of
where to focus and the potential to appreciate
or mourn your current state of manifestation.

By being open to everyone's joy and success, you will better see the potential for your own joy and success.

THE NATURE OF SERVICE

"I choose to serve 'the All' by living in my joy."

Each time you move towards living your dream, any suffering created by you *not* being your dream is released from the world. Know that as you move towards your dream, you constantly aid everyone through your process.

Do not *'try'* to be of service to others purely out of the belief that it is a *'good'* or *'spiritual'* thing to do, as that is to reinforce a belief in right and wrong. The concept of right and wrong is an illusion. It is religion. It is dogma. Instead, know that by walking your own path, you are inherently of *service to all.* You need not *'try.'* You do not need to force anything.

Service is love, and love cannot be forced.

The highest service you can bring to this world is being yourself and living your dream.

This understanding does not mean you do not offer a hand to others when an opportunity presents itself. However, it is also to understand that the best way to help *all* people live their dream is by fearlessness living your own.

Do not let being of service to others prevent you from living your dream — to do so is to diminish your potential and, by extension, the potential of *all* creation. Find a balance that feels good and learn the power to say *"no."* You may have to overcome your fears of rejection and abandonment to do assert this *birthing/unfolding* of self. Put down the baggage from your past, and love will radiate from you rather than need.

> *Do not walk your path for the inclusion*
> *or exclusion of anyone else.*

By knowing how all are connected, step out of inclusion and exclusion as a mental concept behind your choices and feel within your heart when to help another and when to refrain. Do not judge this feeling or apply the morality of society to it. No matter how good your intentions are, if you act against the heart when its guidance says, *"no,"* then you are, at some level, denying joy in the world. To serve others without living your dream is to be a slave.

> *To live fully from your heart is to serve all, in*
> *every moment, without being a slave to any.*

Across our lifetimes, we have all been enslaved many times. You do not need to feel guilty in this life for being free. Beyond genetic heritage is an infinite spiritual heritage that knows no division. *You have been every color, every gender, every sexuality, every everything.* As you come to know this, the lines that separate life will dissolve, and you will see the unity of all.

There is no 'where' and no 'thing'
you have not been.

You are not a part of God — you are God ...
you are whole ... you are included.

CLARIFICATIONS & REFLECTIONS

Our idea of service tends to be attached to a religious concept that teaches us that selfless people are good—*because they serve others*—and selfish people are bad—*because they serve themselves.* This polarized view of service acts as a significant block to following our dream because our dreams are typically deemed to be too selfish and are, because of this fear-based self-judgement, contorted into a *'more socially acceptable'* vision of helping others.

With us all being *the one consciousness...*

All action that flows from
the heart is love.

All love is love for all.

All service is service for all.

All service is *service for all,* even when it looks like you are only serving yourself, because you are an expression of *the all.* You must love yourself first to love anyone else fully. For many people who have been in sacrifice, this is to first service your own desires because that is what has been most untended.

Having opened your heart and found the passion that burns there, understand that the change flowing from your feelings is the desire to create a joy-based world, rather than a desire to patch or remedy the symptoms of a dying, fear-based world. Unless love and joy are our foundation, we will never create a joy-based world (only live in a less traumatic, fearful world).

With so much guilt and shame leading people to serve from a point of self-sacrifice, following your heart is the greatest contribution you can make to the creation of the joy-based world that exists within our collective heart (even though some may judge you to be selfish).

Even with the existence of war and starvation, it is not wrong to dream of visiting the stars in the sky. *We must dream in freedom* to translate and experience the collective shift in our consciousness.

> *Choose to serve your heart as being the ultimate authority in your life.*

This is not because the heart is superior to your mind but because it will lead you to the most joyful and satisfying experiences. It is not that the heart is the *'right'* way and the mind is the *'wrong'* way because it is somehow *'wrong'* to experience separation or disconnection. It is simply that you can choose to experience living through love at this stage in your awakening.

> *Living from the positive is a choice not an obligation, destination, ideal, or rightness.*

ENJOY THE JOURNEY

*"I choose to create space and time
to experience the gifts and rewards
that are present in my life."*

Fears are cages you have used to limit yourself and focus your individuality. As you face each of your fears, you will go through a continual process of freeing yourself from cages — cages that you previously could not name but have always felt. Fears are cages within cages—*mazes within mazes*—and must be faced to experience your spirit in ever-expanding and potentially joyful ways.

*Do not be concerned that as you exit one cage,
you will likely find yourself within another.*

This is your progress through the accumulated baggage of many lifetimes. You will reap rewards for each fear you face and overcome. With each shackle released, you will become ever more fulfilled by better meeting the infinite potential within you.

Celebrate each issue you resolve rather than quickly plowing into the next challenge before you have had time to rest or experience the joy of your success. The rewards of this life are not forced on you; you must pause and focus on them to experience them.

To focus in this way is an
act of loving yourself.

Do not become discouraged by the number of cages you must free yourself from. To do so is to focus on the destination instead of embracing the journey. Learning to *enjoy the journey* is essential for a sustained experience of happiness.

The more you love your life, the
faster its magic will unfold.

As you learn to move with the changes that the resolution of fear brings, you will lower your resistance to your journey. You are here to enjoy this experience, not suffer through it. The only proof of this can come through the living of it.

Although we have created exciting and challenging experiences for ourselves, this is not to say that happiness is the necessary result of their resolution. Even though immense joy may be felt with the completion of a goal, joy is not a reward for achievement.

Having joy as your basis requires a joy-based focus in the present moment. This ability requires the deepest level of clarity, as it is to not be in fear in the moment (as opposed to being calm after mental maneuvering).

Enjoying the journey of your life is
the sum of all your challenges.

To enjoy the journey is to be the self that every experience you designed for yourself points you towards. It is the self that is no longer limited by fear.

CLARIFICATIONS & REFLECTIONS

Although it is true that to comprehend *what awakening is,* you will have lived many lives and will naturally be carrying the encoded baggage of many lifetimes, do not then be disempowered by the traditional concept of Karma.

Karma is a fear-based, religious idea that creates the belief that you cannot escape your past. While it is true that you greatly draw on the experiences of other lives in the creation of your current life (in a way that would seem to honor the idea of Karma), there is no force in existence—*except yourself*—that compels you to resolve events.

Each life is chosen from a state of total freedom; if you find yourself in repeated experiences across lifetimes—*or within a life*—know that you are the one choosing to replay events through your desire for resolution and self-awareness (and not from any obligations created in your past through some 'karmic-law').

As you open yourself to feel peace within the moment, be aware of an opposing drive to achieve, to complete, to bring to order, to clean, to accomplish, to finish, to resolve, to organize, to refine, and to perfect. Recognize these feelings as all being valuable in your creative endeavors, but in this moment of self-awareness, equally recognize the ways in which they do not allow you to be at peace.

*Thank and appreciate these feelings; they bring
great joy when you engage in your passion.*

From this state of appreciation, witness the fearful aspect
of yourself that seeks to constantly engage these *feelings to
become more* (even when you would rather be at rest).

Through this observation, see that what most keeps you in the
feeling of being caught in an unending chase is not a passion
for more experience but the fear-based compulsion behind it.
This fear-based drive causes it to manifest as an unrelenting
master—*the aspect of control*—rather than as a valuable
motivator.

Your passion is one of your most valuable assets and the
source of your clearest potential contribution. But see how,
when you engage it through fear, it ceases to be as joyful.

*Choose to be the master of when you
engage your passion and allow yourself
to rest, free from any pressure to act.*

LET GO OF THE HOW

"I choose to release all preconceptions
of how my dream will unfold."

When calling your dream into reality, do not presume to know *'how'* it will come to be. Your dream may initially appear to be impossible. If you accept this belief, it will be impossible for the duration of that belief.

Not knowing *'how'* your dream will happen is not a limit of the power of your reality to deliver it to you. You do not need to know *'how'* your dream will be possible for it to be possible. You must simply believe that it is possible. This belief in the power of your spirit to create is a profound realization that empowers you not to limit the creational powers of your spirit.

By thinking you must know the *'how,'* you develop the belief that your dream can only arrive in a certain way. To believe in this singular way is to severely limit the options by which your spirit can birth your dream into reality. Focus on your dream and feel it into being without attachment to how it manifests.

Through imagination, experience the joyous feeling of living your dream. This feeling, when deeply connected with can make you feel that your dream is not just a distant possibility but a reality waiting to be lived.

> *Playfully fantasizing about your*
> *dream will draw it to you.*

Simply *thinking* about your dream will not make it happen. You must *feel it with all your being,* and that means surrendering, facing your fear, and letting go of the limiting beliefs you have cloaked your identity in. Start with what you can believe and what you can accept, and work outwards. In this way, you will realize how much it has only ever been you that has hindered the emergence of your dream.

> *The conditions of your reality are*
> *only ever the current manifestation*
> *—and not the cause—of the degree to*
> *which you are living your dream.*

To see this with clarity requires self-responsibility. Have the courage to face the cynic and pessimist in yourself — that voice we call *"the realist."* Understand the ways in which the idea of being *'a realist'* has taken away your hope, out of a fear that having hope will hurt you. For many, this may mean facing their fear and judgment of being perceived as naïve.

> *Dream with the heart of an infant —*
> *a child that has not yet been taught*

by society how to limit its magnificent
fantasy of what this life can deliver.

We have each agreed to participate in this mass consensus reality, but that does not stop all individual realities from being predominantly a personal dream with yourself as the dreamer.

CLARIFICATIONS & REFLECTIONS

When seen clearly, *'to surrender'* does not have a negative connotation. Instead, it means surrendering the ways in which you have been in resistance. This surrender is not a sign of weakness but a powerful tool for personal growth and acceptance of new possibilities.

To surrender is to cease to resist and is most commonly experienced as letting go of trying to control something. We try to control things when we are attached to an idea of how they *'should'* be. To let go of that *'how'* is to allow yourself to experience them *as they are* rather than *as how you think they should best be* (which is a judgment).

Surrender leads to clarity.

Surrender the 'how' of your dream.

As you begin to feel the state of freedom consciousness where you once dwelt—*where anything was possible*—realize that any fantasy can be a reality because that is precisely what each and every fantasy is (a potential blueprint for a reality of a self to be lived).

When we are young, our dreams for life tend to be highly specific, and we can list the details of the career we saw for ourselves, the house we would be living in, our partner, and our lifestyle. As our lives continue to deliver a mix of joyful and challenging experiences that differ from what we had conceived, we start to understand that we are not creating through the definitions of our mental thoughts but through the broader essence of our feelings.

For example, wanting money you had earned, but receiving money as a gift. Wanting an expensive holiday, but instead having more fun on a cheaper excursion with a friend. Wanting to be offered a promotion at work, but instead getting made redundant and moving to work for yourself but then realizing that this is the promotion you wanted (even though it was a difficult experience).

As you see this kind of pattern emerge, continue to dream in detail, but let those details be manifold and fluid. Do not dream of a single way in which your dream must look (because that is to limit it). Instead, dream of many overlapping—*and even contradictory*—ideas that would all feel good to you. In doing so, you will be better describing the potential breadth of feeling of the reality you want to experience. This is to better articulate your fantasy, which creates the clearest potential to step into the living of it.

Imaginatively articulate your
multifaceted dream.

HOW REALITY SUPPORTS YOU

"I choose to see that my reality always supports me in how it exquisitely reflects me to myself."

R eality is your teacher and will aid you whenever you will allow it. The obstacles to living your dream are all of your own creation. No force seeks to hinder or limit you other than yourself (through your choice of unconsciousness). Reality is only ever saying, *"How much will you let me give to you?"*

Accept this idea, and everything will change.

The power of reality to aid you is only limited by your beliefs about *what is possible* and, just as importantly, *what is NOT possible.* In each moment, reality is a powerful mirror of your beliefs.

The only thing you have ever been
fighting for is to love yourself.

When you are caught up in the chase of becoming—*in the chase of trying to make your reality acceptable to yourself*—then you have been fighting to accept the state of your being. Beyond acceptability is joy.

If your reality seems bleak and limited, it is only because it is showing you that some of your beliefs are bleak and limited. It does this with no agenda other than to show you to yourself such that you may become conscious you are carrying those beliefs and may transform them if you so desire.

Embrace the perspective from which *you are your reality* (because your reality is a reflection of you). If you transform yourself, you will change your reality. If you transform your reality, you will change yourself.

Do not accept any belief that says reality
is a prison you are forced to endure.

Reality is a canvas, and you are the painter.

In being a complete reflection, reality is a being … a loving being that is continually showing you to yourself. It is a being because you are a being.

The mirror of reality is you loving
yourself by reflecting who you are.

Many people have forgotten the reflective nature of reality and, instead of changing the reflected beliefs they do not like, they resign themselves to an outer definition they find no joy in and, in doing so, unwittingly choose their own suffering (because they are unable to see a believable alternative).

Reality is a mechanism that supports you by proving whatever you want to believe to be true. If you feel your worth and believe in your dream, reality will reflect it. If you feel unworthy of your dream, then reality has no choice but to confirm that unworthiness and deny you the reflection of your dream.

Reality is not your master; it is best understood as an ally that unfailingly serves you.

CLARIFICATIONS & REFLECTIONS
We each live within the limits of our beliefs. To release limiting ideas of *how* something is possible is to open your mind to possibilities—*which is to say realities*—that are beyond the limits of your mental comprehension. The primary limits of reality are not physical and temporal in the way that we think.

Space-time reflects us; it is not our jailer.

The limits we experience through physical matter and linear time reflect the beliefs that form our mortality.

All realities are created through the belief in what they are.

We purposefully chose for the human experience to have limits because we wanted to define and differentiate it as an experience. As we evolve our understanding of ourselves, we have reflected this through the manifestation of technologies altering the supposed limits of space-time. For example, we can now talk face-to-face through video with someone on the other side of the planet. This technological space-time evolution reflects our spiritual evolution.

*Technology is not separate from spirituality
or heading in a different direction.*

In knowing reality to be a mirror, understand how it reflects your love and care for your well-being such that whenever you feel forgotten or forsaken *'by the Universe,'* you understand that you are meeting the ways in which you have forgotten or forsaken your own well-being. By taking better care of yourself, you are more open to experiencing love and support from reality.

In accepting that we all created reality to be a mirror (such that we could explore ourselves in externalized form), you have to let go of notions that there is anything external from which you can receive love if you will not first give love to yourself.

*No one can 'save you' because there is
nothing you need saving from except
yourself (because of your own negative,
fear-based beliefs about yourself).*

This is something reality constantly demonstrates to us in each moment such that we can choose our beliefs from our heart-based passions rather than the fears that haunt our minds.

*Only YOU can start loving yourself, and only
then will you allow your reality to love you.*

LOVE YOUR BODY

*"I choose to experience my body as a
chosen expression of my spirit — even
if I am experiencing illness."*

D o not see your body as a limitation, for it is not — it is
a gift. Your body is only, in any moment, what you
believe it to be. If you believe your body is degrading,
then so it is. If you believe your body is healthy, then so it is. If
you are ill, then realize that illness is not a mistake or fault — it
has a *purpose/message.* Feel the purpose and allow the illness to
transform your consciousness.

*Everything in your reality is a teacher.
Hear its message, integrate what it has
to tell you, and it will transform.*

You cannot disregard your body and expect it to live in a
balanced way through the polarization of your mind. Feel
your body to be a part of your consciousness. But equally
understand that, as with everything in existence, it can also

be said to have its own consciousness (a reflection of your own gift of *individuality/independence).*

> *Your body is a part of you that has to be*
> *loved and integrated—like every other part*
> *—if you wish to be all that you are.*

Love your body, and it will serve you well. Mistreat your body, and it will let you know (because you will be mistreating yourself). As with all things, it is a question of finding the personal balance that is right for you — the balance between treating your body well in the physical and loving your body with your spirit. These are the same thing because they are reflections of each other.

Treat your body like an old car that constantly needs a kick-start, and that is what it will be. Treat your body as an amazing creation of consciousness, and that is what it will be. The choice is yours because the choice to start loving anything in your life is always with you. The power to love is yours.

> *Your body is yours to love … and nobody else's.*

Once free of your body—*when you leave the experience of physicality at death*—you will remember your physical form as a unique and treasured experience. It is glorious to appreciate your body *now* in this lifetime, rather than waiting until it dies before you realize how amazing your body is.

Allow yourself to know your body. Love touching your body to love your body. Accept it as a part of your unlimited consciousness. Love it as a powerful, reflective extension of your spirit. Your physical form is meaningful — not an obstacle to be transcended. It is chosen. You chose it with purpose.

*Discover the purpose of your body by
loving it as you desire—in your most
intimate place of self—to be loved.*

CLARIFICATIONS & REFLECTIONS

Your physicality is one of the most potent faces of the human experience. Because your body is the most directly identifiable reflection of you (as demonstrated in how we say, *"This is MY body"*), your relationship with your body is one of the most potent relationships you will ever have.

It is a relationship just as significant as your deepest interpersonal relationship. To see your body as something with its own consciousness with which you are having a relationship is to grant it the love and respect you give to the people you most love in your life. For many, this is to elevate their treatment of their body (because so many people have become disconnected from their love and respect for themselves).

*Physical illness within the human experience
is the result of our exploration of separation
through fear-based resistance.*

As such, illness cannot be said to be a *'mistake'* or a *'wrongness'* because our choice to create humanity was not a mistake (unless viewed from within its own fear of itself). This understanding is essential in transforming the energy of an illness because as long as illness is viewed as anything other than a valuable and meaningful reflection, the message of the illness cannot be fully heard.

Furthermore, at this time of awakening, many people purposefully take on physical issues to transform wider issues of self-love and care. The path of transforming an illness requires a level of stepping out of polarity as you seek to love, accept, and allow yourself. This cannot be achieved by viewing the illness as a mistake that needs to be corrected. You cannot *'resist'—through hate or rage—an illness away.*

> *You must transform your experience*
> *of self through love, and that is to*
> *see yourself free of polarity.*

Not all illnesses or disabilities are meant to be cured. In these instances, the path is one of transforming your relationship with the condition until you see why you would have chosen it. In this, the answer is always connected to seeing how the illness or disability has come to transform your consciousness in learning to accept it.

Just as death is not wrong, a mistake, or to be feared, the same is true of illness. Whether you can cure it or not, the path is to love it because it is your choice of experience.

> *No matter how dark external circumstances*
> *may be, see that the choice to pamper your body*
> *through an act of love is a powerful focus that*
> *you can rely on to create a positive experience.*

GIVE YOURSELF TIME

*"I choose to give myself as much time
as I need to make any decision."*

T ime is a construct that reality uses to describe your state of being to you. Lack of time is a feeling ... it is a feeling of lack. When you are in difficulty with any decision, realize the greatest gift you can give yourself is time. If you have not made a clear decision, do not proceed. If there appears to be a time pressure on the situation, understand you are the one creating it and open yourself to the choice to deselect it.

*Open yourself to experience an abundance
of time to make your decisions.*

To allow yourself time is to acknowledge and honor yourself because to decide in haste is to live in fear as a result of doubt being cast by the idea that a rushed decision may have been made. This basis of fear will always have an undesired effect on the outcome, even if it is discovered to be an unfounded fear.

Do not allow the pressure of time to lead you to make decisions until you have reached a point in yourself where you feel confident in your choice. In the meantime, feel confident in the choice of waiting to decide.

To have confidence in your decision is to lead yourself to the intended outcome with confidence (with that intention being the intention of your spirit). Not granting yourself the time you need is a form of giving away your power. At its root is the idea that you are in a reality that has the power to dictate your actions to you. It is to believe there is a force you must defer to in making your decisions, even when you do not feel ready to make them.

In the moment when you allow yourself time, feel that the answer to your decision will be revealed to you. *Feel/imagine* the answer ahead of you, moving towards you. By giving yourself time—*and therefore space*—to make the decision, you will give yourself the clarity you seek. This is a form of allowance.

> *Allow yourself the time you need; it is a gift of energy to yourself.*

Someone who has awoken to the nature of reality while seeing through the illusion of time still uses the experience of time for as long as it is useful. Remember that no decision is forever, as you can always change your mind by changing your perspective. Recognize the power of changing your mind. Do not be afraid to change your mind. Do not be afraid to *verbalize/speak* the change that you represent.

All beings represent a journey of change;
to deny that change is to deny yourself.

CLARIFICATIONS & REFLECTIONS

Regardless of our understanding of time as a mental construct
—*rather than an outward scientific law*—we are all capable
of experiencing time as a form of psychological pressure.
Because we tend to view time as immutable, rushing when
under a time pressure is a logical solution, and we usually
do not bother to question if this reaction is helping us. This
is because moving quickly once served us well as part of the
survival instinct.

It is not '*wrong*' to feel time pressure (just as it is not wrong to
experience individuality). But the invitation of freedom before
you is to become consciously aware of when you are within
that pressure, such that you can make an informed decision
about whether or not the feeling of temporal pressure is aiding
you, versus when it is just being a conduit for expressing your
fear-based beliefs in jeopardy. This awareness empowers you
to manage time pressure effectively, enhancing your decision-
making capabilities.

As we awaken to our wider nature, there
is an opportunity to not experience
jeopardy in relation to time.

This invitation to change your relationship with time is a
choice that you can only meet by being open to change. As
you recognize experience the pressure of time as a choice,
realize the ways in which you can use temporal pressures to
positively motivate you — especially regarding things that
cause you to procrastinate (which is not laziness but a fear-

based reaction to circumstances). Through this observation, sense how extensively we have shaped our experience of reality with linear time. In letting go of the pressure of time, you are stepping into a deeper experience of your sovereignty (because you can no longer blame external factors for your own limits).

Through your growing awareness of the ways in which you have allowed yourself to experience temporal pressure—*by believing you lacked the time you needed*—see how closely this may connect with any financial fears you have. When you open yourself to reality without time pressures, see that the easiest solutions are often financial in nature (literally paying extra to have more time or for something to be done quicker). If you see this in your life, feel your resistance to spending that *'extra'* money. This is to see how many of the time pressures you experience are, in fact, a redirection of financial fears (which are—*at their root*—survival fears).

ACCEPT YOUR CHOICES

*"I choose to experience every aspect of my
reality as being something I have chosen."*

To change your reality, you must become aware—*at the
level from which you are choosing*—of the element
within your reality that you wish to change. This is to
become aware of your original choice for that element. Come
to know why you initially chose what you now do not want
in order to change it. Knowing why you made any particular
choice can best be approached by taking responsibility for—
and ownership of—that choice. Do this by accepting that it was
you who made the choice.

*You cannot change a choice for which
you do not take responsibility.*

This is because the act of rejecting it separates you from that
power. As long as you refuse to believe you could have chosen
a particular element of your reality, then you are the one,
through the focus of that refusal, who is separating yourself

from the understanding of why you chose it. In this condition, you are living in a state of denial and have little hope of changing the choice, except to change its form (which you must still deal with).

To not accept an aspect of your reality is to not accept one of your choices. This is to reject that aspect within yourself. It is not that you must feel joy for everything in your reality, but you must accept that *you created it.* This is necessary if you wish to awaken to yourself as the creator of your reality (which is to awaken to the level of perception of your spirit).

> *Through the power of acceptance*
> *comes the power to change.*

This could be described as a *Catch-22* because it means you must *accept what you do not want* in order to change it into something you do want. Lack of acceptance separates you from your power to choose. To not be accepting of your creation is to deny your choice of reality. All rejection is a form of denial. Remember that denial is not *'wrong'* — it is a choice.

There is no aspect, quality, or thing that does not seek validation through acceptance. Transform yourself through the acceptance and allowance of *all that you are.* Create the potential for transformation in others through your acceptance of them.

> *You have the power to transform*
> *the world through accepting and*
> *honoring all it contains.*

The foundation of acceptance is love. Know that *all seek love.* Recognize your own seeking of love ... find it through the allowance of love in and of yourself.

CLARIFICATIONS & REFLECTIONS

The principal currency of creation is your *focus* with whatever you focus on being that which you give life to (regardless of whether that focus is coming from a place of fear or excitement, and regardless of whether that focus is on something *'real'* in the outer world or something *fantastical* in your imagination).

> *You experience more of whatever you*
> *focus on, whether that be in terms*
> *of qualities, events, or things.*

How this *'creation through focus'* then evolves is determined by your allowance of it versus your resistance to it. Both allowance and resistance are forms of focus and they feed manifestation. Resistance feeds the manifestation of experiences through which you will further feel your resistance. Allowance feeds the manifestation of harmonious experiences.

If you are resistant to certain qualities (through judging them to be negative), then the perception of those qualities in others will continue to grow within your experience. You cannot *'create away'* the elements of your reality that you do not like by rejecting them.

> *Whatever it is you resist will continue to*
> *exist as long as you feel resistance to it.*

To deselect something from your reality, you must first acknowledge yourself as its creator (because this represents the level of acceptance necessary to diffuse the feeling of resistance). What then best leads it to fall into the background of your reality—*where you no longer focus on it*—is the allowance of yourself to be engulfed by your excitement for something else. This understanding is the basis for the powerful teaching...

"Love peace rather than hate war."

By becoming vigilant of where your focus is, and whether it is there for a joy-based or fear-based reason, see the ways in which your life may have been far more fear-based than you realized. It takes time to break ingrained fear-based patterns, but the more you do it, the easier it gets, and you will feel the emotional floor of your reality rising when you no longer allow yourself to overly focus on negative feelings.

Allow yourself to feel what you perceive as negative, accept it as being of your own creation, and release it to exist 'as it will.'

FREE YOUR WILL

*"I choose to experience the infinite
nature of my will."*

There are an infinite number of ways in which you can move into freedom and limitlessness. Just as you can create what you want, you can also deselect what you do not want. When you say, '*"Enough!"* to something, you do not need to consciously see how it should come to not be.

Do not be attached to how you deselect your manifestations. To do so is to limit the ways in which you are open to experiencing change. From your heart, start by thanking what you have had enough of. Wish it well and open yourself to experience a new reality where it is felt and remembered as being of the past. There is nothing that you cannot say *"Enough!"* to.

*To experience the freedom of
consciousness, you must face your*

fears, but there is no set way and no
set time in which you must do this.

There may be many manifestations in your reality that you perceive as negative. Through the process of deselection, you can remove them and create a more joyful world. If you deselect something that still holds a message for you, it will effortlessly re-manifest in a different form.

As you see your reality with clarity, you will learn which aspects are historic, fear-based relics that can be quickly removed and which are current lessons to be explored further. In saying, *"Enough!"* to a current lesson, you will simply create a new vessel for the message. You can shuffle the deck as many times as you like.

Allow yourself this flexibility by
embracing the fluidity of reality.

If you do not understand a lesson in its current form, use this transformative power to change how it manifests. In doing this, you will free yourself from much of the negative history that may have collected around an experience with which you have struggled.

You are not tied to any aspect of
your reality through anything
other than your beliefs.

If you make bond, rather than making them with fear, make them with love and joy. To be subservient to an aspect of your reality is not a *'bad'* thing, as it may well serve you for a while. Just remember—*and take responsibility for*—how you are the creator of your reality.

Your personal inner experience and your outer reality are the manifestation of your beliefs. You hold the ultimate power to choose these beliefs. Free yourself from the mental constraints you have imposed. This journey of self-discovery and awareness is challenging, but the rewards are immeasurable.

*Within you is the power of a
free and infinite will.*

CLARIFICATIONS & REFLECTIONS
Reality is a fluid reflection of a self that you are evolving. It is not an external, fixed, objective challenge to be outwardly solved (although it is not wrong to approach it that way). To understand this fluidity is to understand there are infinite ways in which your reality can convey the experience of your spirit. This is because what you seek is a *feeling* and not a specific *outward definition;* it is not a feeling that can be conveyed in any single static expression.

Ever since *'the one'* became *'the many,'* the consciousness underlying our reality has been within an experience of movement, of blossoming, and of change. Once you have found the sweet spot known as *'being yourself'* (which means fully accepting and embracing your unique qualities and values), reality is capable of eternally translating the beauty of this feeling to you through an *ever-changing/ever-unfolding* experience of self.

*We are each a story of eternal
change, a narrative that is constantly
evolving and unfolding.*

As you start to experience yourself as the creator of your reality—*rather than as being contained within it*—take the opportunity to look anew at the elements of your life you do not enjoy experiencing. Discover how the things you want to let go of have been interwoven with your thought patterns and outward routines. To deselect them, you must open yourself to change ... open yourself to new patterns (both inward and outward).

You are the master of your focus.

You are the master of your energy flow. To deselect something, imagine your new state of focus with such joy that it captivates you. In doing this, let the way you used to view the world start to feel old to you such that you *'leave it in the past.'*

Experience reality as something that arises from your consciousness and not something that you are contained within.

Open yourself to experience a level of freedom beyond any you have known by perceiving the fluidity of what has always been experienced to be solid and immutable. Through this, experience the equality of freedom and limitation ... the equality of the immortal and the mortal ... the equality of the eternal and the ephemeral ... the equality of your spirit and your physical body.

DO NOT FEAR THE FUTURE

"Through inner trust for my life and the knowing that I am the one creating my experience with love, I choose to embrace the unfolding of my future from an empowered standpoint."

D o not relinquish your power to the future by fearing it. Each moment is a product of your energy, belief system, motivation, intent, and inner feeling for *all that you are.* You have spent this life—*and indeed every life*—creating yourself. Therefore, if you are to have faith, have faith in yourself.

Whatever happens to you, you created it to be the highest experience for your journey to know yourself. Even if an experience is perceived as negative, know that you desired it, and it is only your current perception of the experience that is limited.

Within you is the power to see the
reason behind every choice.

Your spirit sculpts every moment of experience from a state of awareness beyond your own (due to your self-chosen limits). Every moment is a perfect expression of your intention for this life. Your human experience is a message to you from your spirit. This message is heard through the choice to consciously perceive your life as a message.

Through this knowing, free yourself from anxiety by holding a deep faith in all events that unfold, as this is to have a deep faith in what your spirit has created for your mortal self to experience. You do not need to fear the future as *what will be will be,* and that will be a perfect reflection. This does not mean your future is predetermined.

It means that nothing is a mistake, all is with
purpose, all is with meaning, and all is of value.

Through the understanding that you are the one creating your reality, do not fear the future. The future is the unfolding of the infinite potential of all creation. It is the unfolding of your mortal self.

If you fear the future, you do not fully trust yourself or your life. Every person can list many circumstances that 'went wrong' to support a lack of trust in their life. Any belief you hold that the negative things you have experienced will unavoidably reoccur creates a fear-based energy that feeds into the creation of your future. This is what creates self-perpetuating beliefs.

Accept and integrate your past.

Realize its purpose, integrate its lessons, and you will free your future from being your past relived. When you do not fear your future, you consciously create your present with love and not subconsciously with your fear. This will collapse the past and future into the present moment, and you will be without regret for the past or fear for the future. To live anywhere but in *the Now moment* is to live outside of yourself.

> *Have the courage to live fearlessly*
> *in the reality that is present.*

CLARIFICATIONS & REFLECTIONS

Our desire to create a confined, limited, mortal experience from the limitless, eternal experience of our spirit can initially feel highly contradictory. Understanding this strange juxtaposition is much of what the journey of awakening to the wider state of consciousness is about.

Each moment of your life is being created from a part of you that you are—*at best*—only partially conscious of. For those who have not had a clear experience of their spirit, to be told that it is from this state of consciousness that the basis of our life arises can feel like you are being told that your future is determined by someone else. This demonstrates not only how *all truth is relative* (according to where you perceptually stand because that creates how you perceive yourself) but also how the perception of freedom is relative.

> *When you awaken, you will perceive yourself to*
> *be freely exploring ideas that you determined*
> *in the creation of your mortal life.*

Your human self is free but within the limits of a feelings-based story that you wrote. This is the understanding that even though you may be in a locked prison cell, you cannot be said to be imprisoned if you retain the key to the cell (even when you choose to forget you have it). In such a situation, the imprisonment is felt to be completely real by the mortal self, but spirit knows it to be an illusion because of its knowledge of the key.

This demonstrates a primary way in which your spirit is perceptually disconnected from the experience of individuality because it cannot perceive the limiting or imprisoning aspects as absolute — only as a free choice in the moment. Despite this disconnection—*which could be perceived as a limitation*—we still call our spirit infinite because *our mortal self is our spirit having a limited experience.*

THE ILLUSION OF EXTERNAL POWER

"I choose to see the polarization inherent in any belief that I need to possess power over anything except myself."

F ree yourself from any ideas or feelings of blaming anyone else for what you are experiencing. To blame another for any event or situation in your life is to enter a state of delusion.

Reality constantly reflects you; obstacles are the manifestation of blockages and fears within yourself (no matter how much another may appear to be creating them).

Know all else—*all others*—as your teachers; another person blocking you is another version of you—*the one consciousness*—in human form, showing you to yourself.

*Abusers and victims are in a dance with
each other — one seeking to take power
and the other seeking to give it away.*

The lesson for both is the same — to stand in their power.
Abusers seek power from a fear that they lack it. Victims give
away their power from a fear of what they will do with it (or
fear of what engaging it will do to them). When either a victim
or an abuser stands in the recognition of their power, then the
cycle of abuse and suffering ends.

See the perspective from which abusers and victims are not
different, and that to see them as separate is to feed into
their belief that they are different (which is a denial of our
shared source). To take sides by denigrating those who believe
differently from you is to reinforce the creation of division
through righteous and judgmental beliefs. This is to enter
further into the polarity yourself.

*Conflict is created by the seeking of
power or the denial of power.*

All participants in a conflict are seeking to find their inner
power. If these power issues are not played out, they will not
be resolved. If they are quelled, they will re-manifest. If one
side seems to be destroyed, it will quickly reappear as a new
army of beliefs.

All external power is *an illusion/a contradiction/a paradox.*
There can never be an *ultimate external power* because power is
not external. Each and every being is inviolate — any belief in
external power is a denial of this. To try to outwardly control
anything *outside of yourself* is to be out of control *inside of
yourself.*

*Do not seek to control abusers
or victims; to not engage in the
polarity, you must unconditionally
love them or leave them alone.*

Live within your own sovereign creation, and the need
to control others will leave you. In releasing controlling
behaviors, you will free unimaginable amounts of energy,
which you can then direct into your dream.

CLARIFICATIONS & REFLECTIONS
In being an infinitely free creator of your reality, you possess
all the power you could ever need to create anything. To
understand that there is only *the one consciousness* is to
realize that if a part of you wants to punish another person,
then an aspect of you wants to be punished. Even though
those two experiences may be across two seemingly separate
individuals, your spirit is fully aware that it is the self within
both experiences.

Karma is not a reward and punishment system for behavior.
It is the realization that you play *both* sides of any drama you
create (because *the one consciousness* plays all roles). There is
no experience—*positive or negative*—that you can perceive has
been inflicted on you that you have not inflicted on another.

*Whatever you do to others, you will
experience as being done to you.*

There is no idea of retribution in this. *What we perceive as two
separate experiences are, in fact, two sides of a single experience.*
This can only be perceived as a limitation by a self within a
judgmental/divisive experience of its own self-creation.

It can understandably feel appropriate to feel anger at abusers and sympathy for victims. No matter how good your intention, this is to engage in and reinforce the *abuser—victim* polarity. In releasing the feeling of blame for how you react to the world, begin to step out of the fear-based cycle of judgment. This will further focus you on seeing how you are the sovereign creator of your personal reality (and so is everyone else).

It can be a challenge to interact with loved ones who express themselves as victims because, once you have had this realization, it no longer feels loving to sympathize with their anger or blame (as it entrenches them and you both further within that polarity). To resolve this is to seek to no longer act as a victim without falling into judging the state of victimhood.

To speak against anything is to be a part of it because it is to enforce the perceptual validity of the separation.

Choose to radiate your joy and empowerment.

SELF-JUDGMENT

*"I choose to experience myself as my
only source of judgment."*

To know *we are God* is to know *we are all one
consciousness.* To know yourself as God is to know *All
As God.* This is to know there is no potential outside
of you that is not also contained within you. You are the
miracle of your beingness. You contain the infinite potential of
expression of *all that can be imagined.*

If you wish to become an embodiment of the dream in your
heart, you must step into your power by perceiving yourself
as the ultimate creator of your life. You alone are the architect
of your reality and, as such, you are the highest-level judge of
what you do. Do not defer your power to choose to any other
being (whether physical or non-physical, ancient, or newly
born).

*Listen to all you feel to, then
decide for yourself.*

*The only clear judge of any decision is
the heart/inner feeling of knowing.*

Even when you do not follow your heart and fall into
suffering, do not then allow that pain to burden you when
you re-enter the stream of joyous feeling within you. Have the
courage to learn from the experience, but then let it go and be
without regret. To live with regret is to be in a limited view of
your unlimited self.

There is nothing 'above' judging you.

Letting go of self-judgment within your decision-making
process can only come from your determination to be without
judgment. No other force or person can make you take your
power because all power is already within you. There is no
higher authority to which you can give this power unless you
choose to create the illusion of it in your mind (for the purpose
of *limiting/focusing* yourself).

*Our giving away of personal power
has been manifested strongly in the
idea of the external, patriarchal,
judgmental God of religion.*

This externalization is the externalization of power through
self-judgment. Many people judge themselves and, in doing so,
externalize their infinite nature by perceiving it as something
separate that exists above them and looks down on them
in judgment. What you may fear as the judgment of God is
reality's reflection of your judgment of yourself. Stop judging

yourself, and you will integrate into your human self the wonder you would perceive as being divine. If you love God now, rest assured you will continue to love God.

> *This is the clearer discovery—not the loss*
> *—of what religion calls "God."*

CLARIFICATIONS & REFLECTIONS

The full experience of reality reflects *all that you are.* You are free to experience each of your many diverse aspects as either internal, external, or existing in both. Because reality is a complete reflection, every aspect must be consciously reflected somewhere. The full creative power of your spirit will always be shown to exist.

> *For each magnificent aspect, if you*
> *cannot believe that you embody*
> *it within you, you must instead*
> *experience it as external.*

Denying something—*to make an element of it unconscious—* does not make it cease to exist; instead, it disguises it within your perception such that you can *pretend* it does not exist. It does not matter whether the aspect is positive or negative — if you deny it as a reality *inside of you,* it will be experienced as a reality that is *external to you.*

If it is a positive quality—*such as your creative power*—then you will feel your self to be inferior to its external manifestation. If it is a trait perceived as negative—*such as your temper*—you will experience yourself as the perceived victim of someone else's temper (upon which you will project a judgment that is really about yourself).

To not accept the judgment of others is a
part of the process of not judging yourself.

In not taking on other's judgments, it is not that you are no longer listening to the world; it is that you evaluate everything for yourself by feeling it from the perspective of your open and flowing heart (that knows itself as infinite in potential).

Your heart will tell you the validity of any belief in relation to your personal path, and when something does not resonate, do not take that to mean that believing in it is somehow wrong for others. Through this process, you will better know yourself because it leads you to understand just how uniquely personal your perspective is

Your life is the journey of unfolding
your unique perspective.

By directly seeing all truth as relative, you will better understand the unlimited power of diversity in relation to the limitations inherent in all who seek to emulate an ideal. Furthermore, you will see how releasing an ideal equally releases judgment of all seen as *'not ideal.'*

Let your projections fall such that you can see
the beauty of your self in the mirror of reality.

TRUST & LET GO

"I choose to flow effortlessly with the currents of my life, knowing they will always take me towards a deeper experience of all that I am."

All trust and faith can ultimately only stem from the self. Your spirit is constantly helping you—*because it is you*—but only as much as your human self will allow. To move forward from the original limited—*but purposeful*—experience of reality you have known, there will be moments when you must consciously and decisively choose to open new avenues in your life. There will also be times to just let go, sit back, and allow the wider perspective of your spirit the space to manifest synchronicities and other such magic (to call it *'magic'* is simply to say that it is beyond our current understanding of how it is possible; it, therefore, appears in a way that feels magical).

Have trust and faith in your wider consciousness to weave new strands of magic and possibility into your life.

Create room in your heart, mind, and consciousness to allow your spirit space in which to move. Remember that your spirit can create *'the how'* of what your heart desires in ways not constrained by the limits inherent in living through logic and rationale alone.

By letting go of the tight reign you may have put on your life, know that you are not *'losing control'* but are exercising the greatest faith in yourself. This is to trust the currents of your life to carry you, by whatever means they choose, to an ever-evolving experience that was specially created—*by you*—for you.

Trust your spirit to constantly, continually, and unconditionally help you become conscious of *all that you are*. This is to know, without doubt, that you are surrounded by love and support (both internally and externally).

Allow your life room to breathe.

If you impose the force of your will on every aspect of your life —*in an attempt to control your experience*—your spirit has little room to maneuver. The greatest learning often stems from letting go and seeing what happens next. This is to know your life as your teacher and it requires letting your experience of reality be your teacher.

When you do not know the answer, let go and let your life speak to you.

To fully let go is to understand that letting go may take you to a beautiful new fantasy beyond your conscious dreams, or it may equally take you to unresolved pain you are in denial of. Wherever you end up, know that it will be where you best need to be to embrace the full experience of *all that you are*.

Appreciate yourself—including your
manifestation as reality—for this gift.

CLARIFICATIONS & REFLECTIONS
The quality of trust is particular to our human self. While it is
not inaccurate to describe it as an aspect of how you feel about
yourself, it is best understood as the feeling that describes
your relationship with *the unconsciousness that defines your
individuality* (even more than how you feel about what you are
conscious of).

Trust is not *"something that is built."* It is our inherent starting
point, but it becomes eroded by the presence of fear (which
can only occur in states of unconsciousness). Your spirit,
being what you are outside of human existence (and outside
of your human unconsciousness), does not have such a
relationship — except through you. It does not experience
trust because *all that is perceived* is trusted equally and fully. In
this, our human experience of trust is seen to be created by our
fear-based experience of distrust.

Trust is a human quality and not directly
a part of our spirit's experience.

As much as you may love feeling the flow of action that
emerges when you are engaged or passionate, be aware of
times when your action flows from somewhere else within
you. This is a place that clearly has the highest intention for
your well-being, but—*unlike your passion*—its perspective flow
from a place of seeking to *avoid things going wrong*, more than
it is seeking *to create what is new and exciting.*

This space within us is wary of new things because they are
feared as not being predictable. It is the space of *fearing the*

unknown. One technique to disengage this flow of fear-based action is, for one month, to choose not to create from any mental basis. Instead, give your spirit time and space to move, free of your fear-based controls.

Stop rowing/choosing/creating/controlling.

Relax and open yourself to magical experiences; follow your heart in the moment wherever it may lead you.

Step out of all mental plans and enter the flow you feel in your heart, externalized as magical streams of possibility that will present themselves to you over these coming days. By doing this, you will be engaging a new open flow of possibility in your life, which you can then balance with the flow of revelation that emerges when you engage your passion.

ACCEPTANCE

"I choose to open my heart to feel
acceptance for all things."

The route to joy lies within the opening of the heart to feel without restriction. Accept the gifts of your heart so that you may realize the joy that is present within acceptance.

Acceptance is not just about having an open
mind; it is about having an open heart.

To accept another person is always to accept a gift (because every person, when met, is a gift). To fully accept and experience the joy of a gift is to stop resisting something that is also part of yourself and let it into your heart (because everything is a holographic reflection of *the one consciousness*).

Many people feel guilty when they receive because they do not deem themselves worthy of receiving. Often, when we receive a gift, we instantly think of what we can give in return that will be of equal or greater value. This is not *'to accept a gift.'* Until you value yourself, you will not be able to receive into your heart and will find yourself separated from the love and joy within and around you. Valuing yourself is the same as accepting yourself. To value yourself is to experience a deep appreciation of the enormity of the gift of your being.

Feel how acceptance is a state of love in that it is through love that we are open and willing to receive the fully conscious experience of life. As such, acceptance leads to the joy of feeling your *unity/connection* with all life.

> *You cannot love and accept another person*
> *more than you love and accept yourself.*

To value another more than you value yourself is to love yourself in the guise of another. What you love about the other person is the reflection of a quality *in you* that you are not feeling inside of yourself. Conversely, know that what you hate in someone else reflects a quality of yourself you are not accepting.

> *Hate stems from a lack of acceptance.*

Support the rights of others, even if they do not seem to apply to you (because in the knowing of connection you will see this to be the illusion of separation). To accept something does not mean you have to want to be it. You can fully accept something that you are not choosing to be. A positive choice does not need to infer the existence of a negative choice.

> *Accept through the allowance*
> *of love in your heart.*

To accept is the choice to allow more of the love you are to flow through your heart, mind, and body.

To accept all is to meet yourself.

CLARIFICATIONS & REFLECTIONS

For an embodied self who has learned to associate their feeling of self with the physical disconnection of their body, the idea of acceptance seems to relate to the acceptance of some *'thing'* that is seen to be separate and external. As such, that acceptance feels optional because there is no sense that a lack of acceptance could be detrimental to the self. Furthermore, the idea of acceptance is felt to be the idea of accepting something *into* your life — meaning it does not feel like expelling something *out of* your life.

There is nothing wrong with this perspective. It is a part of the design of the human experience — meaning that, as an individual, it is desirable to perceive non-acceptance as not detrimental to the self. This is necessary so that the individual can experience defining themselves from positive acceptance —*in which consciousness is promoted*—rather than negative rejection—*in which unconsciousness is promoted*—when they are, in reality, doing both.

Individuality is a state of positive and negative focus—expressed as the separation between consciousness and unconsciousness—which defines a human self within that which is spirit.

Put another way, we do not feel limited by our own lack of acceptance because—*by design*—we are unconscious of what we reject as being *'of our self.'* To begin to awaken to your spirit is to wake up from the perceptual containment of individuality. This is to see how all that you have rejected in the external world as *'not being of you'* is, in fact, equally the denial and suppression of the parts of yourself that they reflect.

For a person who has not first accepted themselves, there is relatively little joy to be derived from the world. Your acceptance of the external world directly reflects your acceptance of your self (the internal).

> *To not accept yourself is to not love*
> *yourself, and that is to live a life you do*
> *not accept, in a reality you do not accept,*
> *from a state of being you do not accept.*

To awaken is to see that unconditional love cannot be for one thing over another because *love does not divide.* Unconditional love is love for everyone everywhere. To feel unconditional love for yourself is to have become all that love is.

"All you need is love."

UNIFYING THE
INNER & OUTER

*"I choose to share my success with others and
to also feel the success of others inside myself."*

Each struggle in your life represents not feeling *'as
one'* within yourself. Just as loving yourself is the same
as loving the world, love is also the path to feeling
unified inside yourself. Breaking down the division in both
the external world and your internal self occurs through love.
When you love a part of yourself that you previously did not, it
becomes unified in your manifestation of the world.

*Love has the power to transform,
to heal, and to unify.*

It is our nature to separate off, within our self, whatever we are
uncomfortable with. Loving yourself is about dissolving these
internal divisions. In parallel, we label and segregate elements

in the external world that make us uncomfortable. These external elements are symbols for the parts of yourself with which you are uncomfortable. Through this understanding, see how the world is a mirror of *all that you are.*

When you break down a division in your view of the world, you will have broken it down inside yourself. Similarly, if you resolve a prejudice internally, you will no longer see its reflected counterpart in your immediate reality. You are a mirror of the whole, and when you act to resolve a division in yourself, you aid all others in resolving it inside of themselves.

> Every personal breakthrough is a breakthrough for the whole.

> Every success in the world is to be celebrated.

> When you feel the success of others as your own, you will discover the feeling of your own success.

> To deeply feel any success is to be within your own success; it can be no other way.

From a perspective, we are already unified—*both individually and collectively*—but we must bring this unification into our state of realization (our conscious reality). When all beings come to love, all existence will become a Unified Diversity. Because physical matter is primarily manifest as a symbol of division, the medium of physicality will become increasingly *permeable/traversable* as we approach this point of Unified Diversity. This will primarily be manifest through technology in how it reflects the integration of our spirit's reality (which is not limited by physical barriers).

Through this permeability, we will transform and manipulate matter in new and exciting ways. Just because this may look like technology does not make this increasing permeability any less magical. Technologies that connect us no matter where we are on the planet are magic.

There is no unity that we must
work together to forge.

There can be no struggle in coming to love.

It already exists.

We must merely open our eyes to it.

CLARIFICATIONS & REFLECTIONS

The spiritual teaching to *"go inside"* is a reaction to most people being predominantly focused on outer survival rather than inner harmony. Despite being so different in sensation, our inner and outer experiences of reality are far more connected than we realize. Their temporal disconnection —*created through the self being translated into linear time*— disguises how the inner and outer are reflections of each other.

To move within your consciousness—
the inner—is to create movement in
both time and space—the outer.

When the whole self is seen in clarity, it is understood that all challenges you create for your mortal self can be approached through either the inner or the outer because both are reflections—*and interfaces for transformation*—of the same thing. Even if the focus is predominantly on one, at the moment of resolution the parity between inner and outer is seen clearly.

What this effectively means that although the approach to any challenge can be focused through either your inner or outer reality, it will always resolve in an experience that represents their meeting (which is the healing of a division—*or denial*—between inner and outer).

> *Stop seeing your outer reality as an obstacle*
> *to overcome, but instead see it as designed*
> *to aid you in knowing yourself.*

By choosing to have a less adversarial relationship with the world, you will become increasingly aware of the beliefs within you that are resistant to this more peaceful stance. In particular, you will become conscious of a web of fear-based beliefs about your financial survival.

If you struggle with finance, you will probably meet an aspect of yourself that, though happy for the financial success of your friends, still experiences their successes as a painful reminder of your own continued struggle (rather than an opportunity to feel and share in that joy). In doing no more than consciously opening yourself to share in their feeling of joy—*rather than letting it make you feel bad by comparison*—you will quickly become a happier person with a brighter outlook despite your finances remaining unchanged.

UNDERSTANDING HATRED

"I choose to approach my reality through the understanding that to love the outer world is to love myself, and to hate it is to hate myself."

Hatred is the manifestation of an internal division that has come to be experienced as an externalized pain through the negative meanings we have labeled it with. This is the result of projecting outward what we do not accept about ourselves.

From a perspective, all hate is a cry for help because hatred for others is an externalization of internal self-hatred.

It is impossible to hate anyone more than you hate the most rejected part of yourself (because all hatred is a projection of your feelings). The degree to which any person hates is the degree to which they hate themselves. Hence, the greater the hatred displayed, the greater the pain the mortal self is experiencing.

What you hate symbolizes something inside you that you are not accepting. You will typcially need to look beyond the surface to identify it.

Some people hate anything they see as representing change, as they do not wish to change themselves.

Some hate anything they perceive as weak because they hate their own weakness and fear being vulnerable.

Some hate all authority, as they fear their own power.

Some hate anything female, as they do not accept their own femininity.

Some simply fear anything different from them, as they feel no security in what they are.

For one person to hate another —*no matter how much that person may denigrate them*—is to see themselves as being a victim of them. The hatred we witness in supremacists does not arise from some *'evil'* within them — it is the manifestation of their belief that they are the victims. It is this belief—*and not the concept we call 'evil'*—that is the foundation from which all extremist behavior stems.

> *To have the courage to see this perspective*
> *is to approach the transformation*
> *of that hatred through love.*

To blanketly write off any person as *'evil'* is to believe peace will only ever come through their execution or imprisonment. This is, however, just another face of the belief that you are the victim who needs protection from that which you believe is your enemy.

Do not attack people who hate—*even though, on one level, this is what they are asking you to do*—as this is to stand with them in hatred (fueling its manifestation in the world).

> *Hate is only transformed through love, and loving someone never looks like being against them.*

> *Love is not against anyone because there is only one self in creation.*

The hatred you perceive in the world can only change within your reality when you bring your love to the aspect of you that hates.

CLARIFICATIONS & REFLECTIONS

Hatred is a negative manifestation of division. Within the human state of polarization, hatred is manifest through the friction and opposition felt between victims and abusers. When seen from this wider perspective, both victim and abuser are seen to be two sides of the choice for a single experience. This experience is chosen for its ability to birth new potentials through the journey of resolving it.

> *Victims and abusers are two polarized perspectives on the same internal issue.*

The degree to which we deny how they are the same—*even though their experience is so radically different*—is the degree to which we deny our ability to be the one whom others may feel themselves to be a victim of.

> *The 'manifestation of evil' is our collective lack of self-love.*

To call a person who has not truly felt love in their life *'evil'* is to be a person who is acting to maintain that person's lack of feeling love. The only experience of evil is the experience that arises out of holding a belief in evil (which is how all beliefs work).

With *'evil'* being a concept created within the human experience, one individual labeling another as evil is the clearest definition of what evil is — meaning *'the conception and application of the label evil'* is what evil is.

> *There was no such thing as evil until religion invented it as a concept to justify oppression.*

You will completely alter your relationship with hatred when you see it as a reflection of your own self-hatred. Whereas ideas of things being *'wrong'* or *'evil'* may have previously been used to be a focus you could righteously express your anger, you will instead experience that anger as a signpost to what you need to love more inside of yourself. In doing this, it is helpful to find new physical outlets through which you can physically express your anger safely from a sovereign place of owning it as the expression of your pain.

When you *own your anger,* you may discover a grief coming up within you to be transformed. This happens because you will no longer be projecting your pain outwards onto others. Talking to friends or a counselor about this will help you to process and release these feelings. It is important to articulate your transformation.

This is not about stopping you from hating—*as you are aiming to integrate your feelings, not suppress them*—it is a process of *owning your pain* instead of believing that others are the cause of it (which is a victim mentality).

FEEL YOUR HATRED TO TRANSFORM IT

*"I choose to experience any hatred I
feel for others as the realization that I
am rejecting an aspect of myself."*

As we begin to understand the nature and origin of our own hatred, it is natural to feel a strong rejection of that hatred wheever we detect it in our thoughts or feelings. However, you cannot hate hatred away. To say, *"I only hate hate,"* is to say that you still hate and that you hate that you hate.

*Hating hate may seem 'moral,' but it is a
judgment that only compounds the hatred
and keeps you trapped in its cycle.*

If what you want is for people to stop hating, then you must love them. If you cannot stop hating someone, leave them alone and look at yourself instead.

Rejecting your hateful thoughts will yield results by breaking you out of repetitive patterns of painful, divisive thinking, but rejection can only take you so far because it, itself, is a form of hatred. While rejecting your hatred is often initially a progression—*in that you are dealing with the issue as being 'of you' instead of 'of another'*—it is just an alteration of form. It does not change the fact thatyou are still creating a painful experience that must be faced if you wish to no longer feel it.

> *You do not need to reject or act against what*
> *you do not resonate with; simply leave it alone.*

While seeking to not hate may seem a worthy goal, do not curb your hatred, as you must meet it and understand *how it came to be* in order to transform it. If we do not acknowledge how we feel then the reason we feel that rejection can never be fully understood. To shine love on hatred—*within ourselves or another person*—is to reveal its root so that it may be healed. It is to provide a space for the recognition of your pain such that through your increased awareness of it, your experience of self is transformed.

> *To hate something is to announce*
> *that you are of it.*

To hate something is to state that it contains something that is within you which you are either rejecting or denying. Demonizing hatred within yourself—*or within others*—can only ever serve to perpetuate it. To transform your hatred, you must love it. To love it, you must see it clearly, which is to feel it without fear of that feeling.

It is in the full allowance and meeting of all your feelings —*whether positive or negative*—that all the life-changing transformations exist.

*To live your greatest dreams, meet your
heart by allowing it to feel everything.*

CLARIFICATIONS & REFLECTIONS

Even though hatred is self-judgment—*and that is self-mutilation*—do not fall into thinking that hatred is wrong, as that is just to hate hate (which is to exist in hatred). Not condemning others who are hateful is a significant step in the journey of awakening to *all that you are.*

Such is the depth of the moral outrage we are encouraged to express—*having been conditioned to believe it is a sign of our civility*—that it can even feel wrong or suspect not to be hateful toward hate. This social-moral imperative to display anger, hatred, and a desire to punish those who harm others —*instead of love them*—is a space into which humanity continues to refine its rejection of the human self. Eventually, it will be understood that the meeting and transformation of this justification for hatred is the same as the meeting of the righteousness that we want to occur in *'the haters'* that we hate.

> The hate of an abuser on behalf of their victim is not different from the hate of a victim for their abuser.

> To hate is to feel divided and is always experienced as some form of weight carried within your life.

> The overall divisive weight of pain in the life of an abuser is as great as that of their victims.

> To hate is the choice to live within division.

Recognizing that feelings of anger, frustration, and superiority are rooted in our own unresolved pain can be a powerful revelation. It allows us to break the cycle of projecting our pain onto others, leading to a state of sovereignty where we *own our pain.* This journey of self-awareness is not only rewarding but further empowers us to understand and accept all aspects of ourselves.

The greater challenge is in choosing how to respond in social situations where friends or associates use their shared anger over an event to unify through their shared rejection of it. Along with not participating in their judgment, it is equally important to not fall into judging or lecturing them. Instead, express yourself through the positive expression of what you believe and support. This could involve sharing your perspective in a non-confrontational manner or redirecting the conversation to a more positive topic.

The key is to avoid defining yourself through the expression of what you judge and reject.

Not hating hatred is the same as not judging judgment.

LOVE YOURSELF

"I choose to give love to myself, knowing that in doing so, I will radiate that love into the world."

When standing at a crossroads in life, one of the most insidious blocks you can put in front of yourself is the idea that there is a *'right choice.'* The idea of right and wrong is one of the most fundamental manifestations of polarization within the human experience. Many strands of thought and negative feeling associations must be unwoven from your belief system to let go of its divisiveness. Free yourself from the fundamentally divisive question that asks, *"Is this better or worse?"* which, being based in perception, permeates all experience.

Whenever you make a decision, use it as an opportunity to observe the origin of your thoughts.

Are you listening to your heart?

Are you listening to society, your parents, or friends?

Are you listening to your own internal concept of right and wrong?

Are you listening to what you believe would make you a *'good'* or *'spiritual'* person? Are you looking to fulfill the wishes of others and ignoring your own needs?

Be conscious of what *forms/informs* your decisions. Learning to observe your mind while standing on the point of freedom of a choice will reveal any psychological baggage you are still carrying. It is to learn to see the filters—*resistances, obligations, and denials*—through which you create your reality.

Embrace the freedom that comes with making choices from your heart. Only when you first love yourself can you truly radiate love, and only then can you fully create space for others to share in that love. Make your choices from your heart without fear that this is selfish.

> *The love that created all life is bountiful;*
> *your heart is of that love.*

At times, your heart—*through the feeling of guidance that flows there*—will guide you to stand in front of others to fill your cup first, and at other times, it will ask you to act altruistically. Trust that whatever your heart tells you is—*because it is guidance from a wider level of understanding*—for the benefit of all (even when it tells you to put yourself before others through an action that others may deem selfish).

> *Love for self is not just a personal journey;*
> *it is the foundation of love for all.*

> *Your self-love has the power to*
> *shape a more loving world.*

See the perspective from which *love for self* builds *love for all* and, conversely, how *love for all* can be used as a denial of *love for self*.

> *Love for all without love for self is running*
> *... running from what you feel yourself to*
> *be (no matter how noble it feels).*

All freeing choices start with love for yourself. It is the key to unlocking your true potential and living a life of freedom.

CLARIFICATIONS & REFLECTIONS

The belief in right and wrong creates the experience of judging everything through a lens of questioning, *"What is better and what is worse?"* One of the most camouflaged manifestations of this perceptually divisive belief is the idea that certain actions, behaviors, thoughts, or feelings are selfish and are to be judged harshly. In contrast, others are selfless and to be judged positively.

With so many pleasurable experiences being labeled as selfish, *"I am selfish"* has become a conceptual whip—*formed through religious doctrine*—with which many people regularly torture themselves. The freedom to put down this painful belief is the realization that all experiences that arise from following your heart birth from a level of consciousness that *knows itself as all*. This is the level of your spirit — your infinite self.

> *The personal feeling of direction you*
> *receive through your heart—which may, by*
> *conventional standards, read as selfish at*
> *times—comes from a vantage point that is*
> *inherently loving and honoring of all.*

As you seek to better love yourself, you will be faced with how much you judge yourself. See how these are the same ways that you have judged the world. See how there is no difference between them. We each live within the restriction of our beliefs around *'how things should be.'*

The solution to this is clear. You must love and accept yourself *as you are* and the world *as it is* if you wish to live in freedom. Do not love because it is moral, spiritual, or *'the right thing to do.'*

> *Love because you want to live in a reality*
> *that reflects the joy and freedom inherent*
> *in all that is created from love.*

Once you have released the question of whether or not what you want is selfish, you will find yourself considering many new exciting avenues. What makes any heart truly joyful cannot be selfish. This will be clear when you see how infectious your joy is to the people in your life who are open to enjoying life.

JUDGMENT

*"I choose to know my judgments as
being of myself and not of others."*

Y ou choose what you believe. This can be done with
or without conscious awareness. To do it
unconsciously is to act from your existing beliefs
through which you avoid—*separate yourself from*—anything
that causes you pain. This leads to wounds becoming
entrenched as beliefs in limitation. However, if you form your
beliefs with conscious awareness—*according to your heart and
not mental logic*—then you will be drawing from the infinite
state of wisdom within you.

*Only you have the power to act from
the consciousness of your heart and
not from the unconsciousness inherent
in your fear, hurt, and wounds.*

With the realization of your power over your beliefs comes
understanding the redundancy of judgment. To judge another

through the projection of a painful feeling is to repeatedly experience the pain the judgment represents across the entire experience of life.

We each live within the feeling of our judgment.

To judge another is to seek to externalize your pain through the illusion it is being carried by someone else. This is not something to reprimand yourself for; it is the way of the reality in which we have chosen to exist.

Beyond judgment is love.

Judge, and you will live in a reality of beings from whom you feel separate.

Love, and you will live in a reality of beings you feel close to.

To love yourself is to cease to judge yourself.

To stop judging yourself is to see yourself, the world, and their connection in clarity.

You cannot control whether or not you feel judgment. What you choose to do with that judgment is the creative choice that steers your life. Use it to know yourself more clearly, and you will move into ever-expanding freedom. Deny your part in it, and you will fall further into the maze of living within a reality bounded by externalized pain.

When you judge other people, you become surrounded by those very people (until you acknowledge the pain they represent lies within you). This is not *'the universe'* punishing you — it is your reality loving you. It is your spirit creating the potential for you to end your suffering by showing you the pain you are carrying.

Instead of feeling guilty for any
feelings of judgment you may have,
use them to free yourself.

Your judgments are messages of
your unresolved pain.

CLARIFICATIONS & REFLECTIONS
Although you are the only one who chooses what you believe,
this does not mean you necessarily know the unconscious
beliefs from which you create. Everything you experience
is a mass of information being integrated into your belief
system. This happens predominantly through a cumulative
translation of feelings into beliefs but also through mental
ideas you choose to adopt directly as your personal truth.

Reality is a mirror, and its response
to all beliefs is the same.

With the impartiality of a mirror, it simply says, *"This is what
is."* Doing this reflects what we believe in. We have created this
reality to be our constant teacher in how it shows us what we
believe through the experience of self that results from those
beliefs.

Your body, the human species, and the planet Earth are not
objective things that are separate from you. They are best
understood as ideas because, experientially, they are what you
believe them to be. They are ideas that arise from your beliefs
and, in human form, you live in relation to them. If you alter
what you believe yourself, the planet, or humanity to be, you
will alter the reality you are living within.

This is how creation through belief works.

In realizing that your negative thoughts are all reflections of your pain, you will reframe your own judgments as not being hateful of others but as being hateful of yourself. What may have initially felt like personal shame around your judgmental thoughts will then be seen as a form of grief because of your acknowledgment of the hurt and anger within you — pain that is connected to past events you have not fully come to terms with. You will then work directly on these unresolved *wounds/events/relationships* rather than on their manifestation as anger, righteousness, and judgment.

Recognize your negative thoughts as a further opportunity to clear yourself of any remaining emotional wounding you are carrying. In doing this, your experience with them will no longer be negative.

DO NOT WORRY

*"I choose to deal with my wounding
directly rather than through
being a fearful person who
worries about the future."*

Worrying—*unlike constructive problem solving*—is an expression of fear. It has many colors, from self-punishment to the cross-wired belief that you must be a particularly caring and worthy person to spend so much of your time worrying.

*Worrying is an intellectual extrapolation
of a physical survival instinct
that no longer serves us.*

The action of worrying is the giving of your energy to your fears and, as such, serves to manifest—*rather than prevent*—them. To worry is a demonstration of a lack of trust in yourself.

Letting go of worry is liberating. It's about relinquishing the need to control your reality and facing your fears head-on, rather than hiding behind the guise of justified worry. Choosing not to worry is a powerful tool for identifying and releasing fears, allowing you to surrender to the natural flow of life, which is to trust in yourself. Following this path, guided by your inner compass, will lead you to greater freedom.

Worrying is an expression of fear through which we try to control our reality from the perspective of pain avoidance.

To worry is to define yourself from a definition of pain rather than joy. Worrying is currently the most pervasive form of fear-based expression in the world, and if you give it your power, then that power will contain and limit you.

Remember, you are in control of the thoughts you give energy to. Do not be hard on yourself for having worrying thoughts, as this only adds to your discomfort. When you notice yourself focusing on worrying thoughts, let them go. This practice will bring up the fear behind your thoughts, allowing you to work with that fear directly (rather than indirectly through worry. Be kind to yourself).

Free your mind from worry. Do not fear that not worrying is living in delusion or idealism. To not worry is to live in total inner trust, joy, and love.

Choose to be spontaneous over worry.

Choose love, not fear.

Worrying does not solve problems.

Worrying solves nothing.

Love and nurture whatever it is
that you wish to transform.

CLARIFICATIONS & REFLECTIONS

Often, we use ideas that are presented as reasonable and logical to disguise feelings we are uncomfortable with. For example, there is a pervasive belief that worrying is better than not worrying because of the rational argument that we are focusing on finding a solution; however, in most cases, we just stay within a circular train of thought that feels bad.

A negative feeling is an alert to stop for
a moment and seek a greater awareness
of whatever is feeling bad.

This feeling indicates you are moving away from what you want to create rather than toward it. This is why you need to be conscious of your feelings to be fully conscious of your beliefs. Do this, and you will become a conscious master of your belief system, instead of an unconscious, anxious, fearful victim of your wounds.

To become conscious is to face and
resolve your pain/feelings.

The journey of releasing the act of worrying from your life will take time because of how worrying can become so ingrained in our daily thought processes. To begin with, you may find yourself deep in worry before you catch yourself. When this happens, do not berate yourself. Any behavior built over many years will take time to shift. When you find yourself worrying, instead of chastising yourself for how anxious you may already be, praise yourself for becoming conscious of the negative thought loop.

Next, actively focus on holding a positive view of whatever you are worrying about. Do this by imagining multiple ways the situation could be resolved and even evolve to your benefit. Through this process, slowly but surely, you will find yourself worrying less and catching yourself quicker when you get anxious.

> *One key to resolving this pattern is not*
> *viewing worrying as the enemy.*

Allow your transformation of worry to be a rewarding process as you feel your shift in perspective from being worried about the future to being a person who embraces change through a deep trust that arises from knowing yourself as the creator of your reality.

JEOPARDY

"I choose to know myself as the creator of all experiences of jeopardy in my life through the choice to experience the intensity of something I am attached to really mattering."

Life is an ever-evolving story constantly creating itself. This could be imagined as the idea that you are in a movie that you are simultaneously directing and watching. What you fundamentally are—*consciousness*—is as safe within humanity as you are safe from being physically harmed when watching a movie.

There is no jeopardy at the level of your spirit because it understands itself to be the free creator of its own experience.

To your spirit, all that you experience as jeopardy is seen to be the result of an illusion (a delusion that *'the illusion is real'* created by unconsciousness).

To not see jeopardy negatively, it is important to recognize that as much as you like to feel safe, you also enjoy feeling jeopardy. The enjoyment you derive from experiencing jeopardy is one of the reasons you sometimes choose to go deep into the illusion of being separate from *the one consciousness.*

Explore the qualities of danger through which you experience joy, so you may better choose when you want— and do not want—an experience to go into the feeling of jeopardy.

You are now, if you so desire, exiting the experience of perceiving jeopardy as purely a negative thing. With these words, you are welcomed into reality, where you no longer find yourself contained within fear-based experiences of jeopardy.

You are consciousness, and you are not only safe ... you are immortal. The immortality of your consciousness as a potential gateway to the knowing of safety.

Nothing external can touch the conscious awareness that you are.

To exit jeopardy is to recognize how your prior fear-based experiences of danger were, in fact, intensely focused experiences of the fear. To be awake is to know and take ownership of your attachments. By extension, this is equally to take responsibility for the jeopardy and drama associated with them (which is experienced as the shadow side of the positively-charged intensity of connection created by the attachment).

Through the focus of your mind, you can experience any state of being you desire (including those based on the illusion that you are somehow in danger). *Enjoy jeopardy, knowing you are safe.* See the paradox of this and simply choose to allow the feeling of safety. Jeopardy is but an option you can choose to express your fear.

> *Allow the experience of danger to reveal*
> *—rather than cloak—your fear.*

CLARIFICATIONS & REFLECTIONS
The human experience is a multi-dimensional illusion that allows your spirit to create the illusion of jeopardy within the experience of a human self. Jeopardy is not a mistake. It is only through a purposeful, intense focus that the experience of jeopardy is created.

> *Jeopardy is not some 'thorn of this*
> *reality' that needs to be removed.*

Through a process of awakening, which involves becoming conscious of your attachments and taking ownership of them, you can alter your relationship with jeopardy such that it becomes an empowered choice to consciously experience a feeling of danger (instead of being a destabilizing experience that reflects the unconsciousness of your own wider nature).

By becoming conscious of attachments within you that may have previously led you to fear-based experiences of danger, jeopardy instead becomes a strongly focused feeling of excitement you can get caught up in the illusion of — such that there is an extra edge of intensity and thrill added to the experience.

Jeopardy can carry the positive association of being an extension of the experience of excitement.

Jeopardy is not eradicated through the awakening of your spirit's wider perspective. Instead, the relationship with the illusion of danger is altered to be an invigorating—*rather than fear-invoking*—experience. What is let go of is the experience of jeopardy as an extension of fear.

Roller-coaster rides are an example of jeopardy being used to extend the feeling of excitement.

These kinds of rides are thrilling because the feeling of jeopardy is powerfully associated with the feeling of fear (and the association is triggered). This is how, even though the brain logically knows that roller-coasters are relatively safe, there is still an intensely *'real'* sense of danger felt during the ride.

With an awakened consciousness, you have the power to disarm any fear-based illusion of danger while still maintaining the choice to consciously allow yourself to *'get caught up in'* exciting joy-based illusions of danger which are experienced as temporary (which is to say, *'of the moment'* instead of *'of the self'*).

FREEDOM IN TIME

*"I choose to acknowledge any
constraint I experience within my life
as being of my own creation."*

R eality is not a race to achieve or create something.
There is no ticking cosmic clock except that which
you create to measure and judge your rate of
evolution against. Feeling under pressure is a form of giving
away your power. To believe you are fighting against the clock
is to live in fear that you may not arrive *'in time.'*

There is no 'in time' to arrive in.

You can arrive at *any time,* or you can arrive from *outside of
time.* You will arrive when you arrive, and when you arrive, it
will be perfect. To arrive and then anxiously check the clock
is to knock yourself out of the present moment into a state of
self-judgment.

*By awakening to your spirit, you
can become a master of time.*

You can even create *extra time* when you need it. In any moment, feeling yourself to be *against time* will instantly take you into a reality where you are facing an opponent — against whom you will either win or lose. Let go of this concept of time, and you can only win. This act of letting go is not a defeat but a liberation.

You are free to enjoy the jeopardy created by competitively racing but do so with the understanding that if it starts to cause you worry or pain, you can stop and *take your time*.

> *Being open to change is no more about being*
> *open to large amounts of change than it*
> *is about being open to small amounts.*

The dream in your heart is not about achieving some level of quantity (quantity is part of the illusion of competition). When following your heart, the finest adjustments to your course are potentially as powerful as the largest shifts. Sometimes, a giant leap will bring you into the greatest appreciation of the interconnectedness of life, while at other times, just a small adjustment will unleash the greatest freedom.

> *You are not in competition with any*
> *other being, for you are all beings.*

Any concept of *'being in a race'* is an idea created by you to be against yourself. The feeling of jeopardy arising from competition can be desirable in the moment; however, if the rush of adrenaline turns to fear, you have the power to let it go. Appreciate the perfection of the present moment.

> *The next moment will be perfect*
> *whenever you arrive at it.*

Transcend the boundaries of
time by allowing time.

CLARIFICATIONS & REFLECTIONS

As you awaken to a wider state of existence of your spirit, you will realize you have predominantly experienced time to be an external, immutable quality over which you have no power—*the scientific view*—because that is how we—*as spirit wishing to experience human form*—intended to experience it (due to how it helps form a deep level of individuality through separation). However, it is possible to transform your beliefs about time such that you have a relationship with it that is far more empowering.

We have used the experience of time to
shape our experience of the human self.

You can alter your relationship with time to be its master rather than its prisoner. The initial face of this realization is seeing how your feeling of urgency is a translation of a fear-based belief in jeopardy (with the limits—*usually interpreted negatively*—and resultant focus—*usually interpreted positively* —of which you have been choosing to experience).

The sense of being in a race against time has always been a powerful experience. We often use a sense of urgency to help us get things done. There are also positive reflections in certain games where it is enjoyable to compete not only with each other but against the clock as well — such as seeking to beat our personal best time. Along with these positive reflections, there are many experiences where feeling rushed is felt as stressful and detrimental.

It is important to be conscious of whenever that pressure affects you negatively. Do not seek to never feel time pressure; seek to be fully conscious of all aspects of your relationship with time.

Being a master of time is not about completely letting go of the sense of time pressure.

One way to begin this is to observe how easy you find it is to stop and relax for an extended period. This will make you conscious of any anxieties you may still carry around time, as they tend to come to the surface whenever we do not feel we are being productive. Use this technique to reveal if there is a deeper level of 'chase' within you.

Everyone has a relationship with an inner feeling of chase.

PERCEIVING FROM THE POSITIVE

*"I choose to maintain a positive
perspective on whatever I
am experiencing."*

Make your choices from the perspective of choosing joy instead of coming from a place of pain avoidance. This is the same as saying, *"love peace rather than hate war."* If you can free yourself from judgment enough to do this, it will transform your experience of reality (because you will be defining your life from a positive—*rather than fear-based*—outlook).

This standpoint is not about denying negativity — as that is to be in fear of it. There is value in the experience of everything you have created. By looking at what may initially feel to be negative from a positive perspective, you will transform your experience of it. This ability is revitalizing and liberating as it represents the empowered choice to free yourself from fear of the negative.

*Allow yourself to feel your pain to
hear its message and release it.*

*When allowing your pain, be conscious
not to elongate it into suffering by coming
to define yourself by it/identify with it.*

Though your pain reflects what you are currently experiencing, you are only defined by that pain if you choose to make its existence a part of your self-identity. Do not identify who you fundamentally are with your wounds.

Allow your pain, forgive yourself for creating whatever experience led to it, and release it into transformation. This can be a beautiful experience of *release/putting down your baggage.* It is only when you define yourself by that pain or become attached to it from the desire to express the victim role that pain becomes entrenched as suffering.

*Guilt and shame create beliefs that
elongate pain into suffering.*

Look at your beliefs about any pain you are feeling to see if those beliefs are aiding the release of your pain or holding it to you. If you feel your pain as anger, express it as anger. Wherever anger takes you—*or someone else*—is where you are both choosing to be. To judge your anger is to deny the experience you have chosen. It is to deny a part of yourself and live in separation from *all that you are.*

Love and anger are not incompatible.

Angry feelings can be expressed in love. Allow yourself to express any anger you feel in order to assert, experience, and understand your own boundaries — as well as how they create your feeling of self. Anger does not need to attack, but even if it does, even if that is how it bursts out, have faith in yourself that you are creating an experience for the benefit of all involved.

*Trust in—rather than judge—
the expression of your life.*

CLARIFICATIONS & REFLECTIONS
The quickest, simplest, and most effective way to make your reality feel better is to view it from a positive-feeling perspective rather than a negative-feeling one. Though this technique is simple to understand, it is not simple to implement because you must face the part of your belief system trained to be *'a realist'* rather than a creator.

A shift to a positively orientated perception, when undertaken by a person who has consistently lived within a negative orientation, is a life-changing experience because it represents a journey of redefining most of what you have experienced yourself to be.

Logic tells us that changing the orientation of our perspective does not change our outer reality, only our perception of it. It tells us that to focus less on the negative viewpoint is a state of denial rather than empowerment. This is certainly logical within the scientific framework (which is a way of understanding the world based on observable, measurable evidence). But this is an understanding of reality that continues to deny how the expectation of the observer alters the objective measurement of reality.

Only you can prove this to yourself by challenging the validity of *'the realist'* within you. The *'realist'* is the part of you that believes in the objective measurement of reality, the part that thinks in terms of what is *'real'* or *'possible.'*

By being open to the magic that unfolds when you shift to a more positive focus (the term *'magic'* here being the name for what we have yet to intellectually understand), you can challenge this mindset and open yourself up to new possibilities.

You are not your pain.

Your pain is a part of your exploration of self.

Because what you fundamentally are is free—*and not in a state of pain*—your pain can be resolved through your journey to be *all that you are.* This pain—*including the journey of its resolution*—is not some by-product of your spiritual exploration; it is your spiritual exploration. You are not bound by your pain but are on a chosen experiential journey to heal it.

Your pain is a defining facet of your self-created spiritual journey.

Through this understanding, transform your relationship with pain. Instead of seeing it as a mistake or sign you are failing, see it as a wise choice you are making from the level of your spirit (which is you with a much wider vantage point). It is notable how much less pain you will feel by accepting your pain, instead of constantly battling to be free of it (which is to say, separate from it).

RIGHT & WRONG

NO DECISION SAVES
OR DAMNS YOU

*"I choose to live through my feeling
of preference in the moment rather
than in relation to mental plans."*

The journey of awakening can be described with many varied terms and approached in many ways. At some level, it is always the stepping out of an aspect of perception that was created to polarize your experience of life by separating how you label its qualities.

To understand that our perception does not have to be polarized is to see that the idea of right and wrong is not something intrinsic to our reality but is, in fact, a twist in our perception that *we have chosen* to live within the experience of. With this knowing of self, free yourself from the concepts of *right and wrong* and the more subtle, insidious concept of *better and worse.*

When reality presents you with a choice, and it does not seem clear which road to take, do not get caught up in the belief that there must be a right and wrong path. Free yourself from the idea that one path must be *'the best'* (the ideal). To think in such terms is to create a reality where you are in jeopardy ... in a reality where choices are tests and—*depending on your answer*—you will be led to either a good or bad consequence.

Being polarized is not how the human experience needs to be. It is only ever you who makes it feel this way when you assign labels of right and wrong—*or better and worse*—to your choices. The human experience is not inherently negative.

> *You assign the meaning through*
> *which you experience reality; it is*
> *not the other way around.*

When faced with a difficult choice, think of all options as leading to positive outcomes. Imagine all outcomes as containing aspects of joy, see how they are different, and select the one you want based on the feeling of preference in your heart — not on the logic of your mind.

Once you have decided, feel joy and confidence in your decision. Do not give your power away to doubt or fear of your decision. In a world without the belief in good and evil, there is neither salvation nor damnation — there is only being.

> *No decision can either save or damn you;*
> *there is no such thing as a mistake.*

Trust in what you have discovered yourself to be to free you from the need to judge yourself or the choices you make. Be free to consider all options presented by your choices. Your will would not be truly free if right and wrong choices existed.

Meet yourself in freedom to see through
the illusion of right and wrong.

CLARIFICATIONS & REFLECTIONS

The feeling that our choices are tests through which we lead ourselves to better or worse experiences of reality creates a complex set of emotions. These are encapsulated in the feeling of regret. To see a choice you have made with regret is to not see the choice, its result, or yourself clearly.

The feeling of regret can only ever result
from some level of unconsciousness.

We—*as the one consciousness*—become human for the experience of it. It is not something done with a defined purpose. Being human is the evolution of our spirit through a focused experience. This evolution is always achieved because you cannot help but be changed by your experience — all change is evolution.

This is equivalent to the understanding that you cannot make a mistake observing yourself in a mirror. However you see your reflection, whether you label it beautiful or ugly, spiritual or profane, is always the most pertinent way for you to perceive it. Even if what you see is negative or painful, that reflection is of an energy within you coming forward to be seen, known, and transformed.

Labeling the result of that observation as 'a
mistake' is the act of someone resisting the
change for which they, themselves, are reaching.

The feeling of judgment and the feeling of the qualities we label as negative are closely linked (recognize how they feel similar). In our exploration of the positive qualities we seek to embody, we tend to reject whatever we see as being their opposite.

> In seeking to live healthily, we judge people we deem unhealthy.

> In seeking to be happy, we judge unhappiness to mean that someone is failing (because that is how we judge it in ourselves).

> In seeking to be kind, we harshly judge cruelty (as if we have never been or felt cruel ourselves).

This is a denial, as we know ourselves to have—*at least sometimes*—expressed both sides of all the polarities through which we perceive life.

> You do not need to judge cruelty in order to be kind.

> You do not need to judge hatred in order to be loving.

> The key here is to see that whatever you judge in others is also a quality of you.

*Only through not judging others
can we not judge ourselves.*

SHINE YOUR LIGHT

"I choose to shine my light unashamedly."

Inside of you is light. This light is the feeling of your spirit and shows you what it feels like to be without fear. To express this light is to embrace *all that you are* because it is to cease resisting yourself. To hide from the light within you is to hide from the magnificence of yourself and its expression through the dream in your heart.

Shine your light.

Shine bright.

Shine unashamedly.

Many say, *"Who am I to shine? Who am I to stand out as different when we are all one? If we are all equal, how can I feel special?"*

*Do not be afraid to stand out in
the expression of your light.*

Do not fear how this may make you feel different, even though being different may have led to suffering in other lifetimes.

*Your history does not need
to repeat itself.*

If you can release the roots you formed in fear and embrace the change that shining your light will bring, then that light can only bring you joy.

We fear the world will tear us down for being so egotistically presumptuous and arrogant as to shine. This is a redirected fear of our light — much of which may be stored within the very cells of our body (from both childhood and other lives).

Enter your body fully and exist in it.

Feel love within it, and you will release these painful, cellular memories.

Know with all your heart that unashamedly being yourself without restriction will bring you joy, and your knowing will be your experience.

*Through each of us shining our light,
we will all connect as one.*

Shining our difference—*not our sameness*—will unify us internally and externally. What once may have made you feel different will be what makes you realize we are all one. In accepting what you are rejected for, you will discover the acceptance of all. Through the embracing of your alienation comes unity. Only by standing fully in the light of your mortal self will you discover the direct experience and knowing of *'all as one.'*

Feel the one consciousness within all by feeling that which connects all.

Live in the knowing of that harmony. Do not fear your light. Do not fear yourself. Your light is that which is carried eternal. It is the infinite existence you have willingly denied in your exploration of humanity. It is time to meet your spirit. It is time to meet your light.

Feel your spirit to feel yourself.

CLARIFICATIONS & REFLECTIONS
Phrases like *'the light within,' 'your inner divinity,' 'following your heart,'* and *'being open to magic'* can make those within a scientific mindset uncomfortable because they are not easily defined — like the word *'consciousness.'* However, just because something is not easily defined does not mean it does not exist — *'being in love,'* for example.

So sure is religion that it is based purely on the knowing of God, and so sure is science that it is based purely on the knowing of physicality, that neither mindset acknowledges how they are the opposing ends of a polarized quality of self.

Scientists are keen to distance themselves from the types of thinking they judge harshly but rarely perceive how a significant part of their self-definition is based on a rejection of the religious mindset. This is manifest in an instant rejection of anything that cannot be quantified without consideration of anything that reflects it. In doing this, science has entrenched its devotees in an experience of reality that does not allow their feelings to offer guidance or the acknowledgment of synchronicities as both magical and meaningful.

> *Those who are scientifically or*
> *religiously polarized must put down*
> *their judgment of each other if they*
> *wish to experience all that they are*
> *— the full spectrum of their being.*

The transformation of humanity into a conscious *Unified Diversity* does not occur through celebrating our sameness and repressing our differences — it can only ever arise through celebrating the richness of our diversity and the idiosyncratic intricacies of our life's tapestry.

YOUR RESPONSE TO SUFFERING

Author's Note: Even though this text only explores the logical conclusion of the idea that we are each the creator of our own reality, it can still be challenging to read. The realization described is only being offered for you to consider applying solely to yourself. It should be met in the wider context of seeing the importance of fully accepting that you are the creator of your reality (if you want to integrate the perspective of your spirit). This concept is being misunderstood if you use it as a tool to disregard the suffering of others as not being of your concern. *We are all one.*

"I choose to take responsibility for my suffering."

To be *all that you are* is to stand in your power of choice as a creator-being. It is to recognize yourself as the creator who shaped your reality. The realization that you are the architect of the suffering you've endured may initially shock the wounded self within you and may take time to fully integrate. Do not rush the process, but allow it to unfold at your own pace.

Give yourself the space
and time to do this.

At certain points in your life, you have *represented/made* the choice to suffer. This means that if you are suffering now, you are, in this moment, choosing to suffer. Allow yourself to feel angry at being told this, but also know that as scary as this concept is—*and as angry as it may make you feel*—allowing this realization is the doorway out of suffering and into creatorship.

Realizing that you have been the creator of your own suffering is a liberating revelation. It signifies that just as you have the ability to create suffering, you also possess the power to un-choose it. To un-choose something is not to obliterate it but to cease giving it your attention. The first step is acknowledging you were the one who created it (such that you can stop choosing it).

No matter how much you have raged over
your suffering or cursed existence, neither
you nor anyone else needs to be forgiven.

To feel anger at your own suffering is a part of the process of taking your power back from it. If you still feel there is a need for forgiveness, then realize *it is you that you need to forgive.*

You have not done anything wrong
— it is not wrong to suffer.

The idea that to suffer, you must have done something wrong was adopted to make the idea of suffering feel like an understandable—*and therefore acceptable*—consequence. However, it also became a mechanism of control (predominantly by organized religion).

Release any concepts of fault or blame you still foster within you to clearly see what suffering is. At the heart of this realization is the acceptance of your right—*and the right of others*—to suffer. Do not fear the acceptance of any quality—*do not fear anything*—for you are the creator of all you experience.

> *There is nothing to fear to except*
> *yourself and to fear yourself is not to*
> *see yourself yourself clearly.*

CLARIFICATIONS & REFLECTIONS

The idea of ending or destroying something—*such as suffering*—is the desire to separate yourself from it by putting it *in the past.* This experience of eradicating something from your reality can only occur within a self within the illusion of linear time.

To awaken and become *all that you are* is to embrace the knowing of your spirit, which is to have stepped out of the illusion of separation. This is to not only realize that you cannot destroy anything—*because it is all a reflection of you*—but that everything you have ever experienced still exists. This is the reality-shifting realization that you have never truly left behind, destroyed, extinguished, or separated yourself from anything.

> *Your spirit within you knows itself to be*
> *the creator of its own experience.*

The teaching that *'you are the creator of your own reality'* is not some naïve, fantastical invitation to ultimate power. It is a confrontational invitation to take responsibility for everything within your experience, regardless of whether you perceive it to be positive or negative.

The call to *'shine your light'* is also a call to meet and hold your own darkness. Just as spirit exists within you, so does your wounded self (also known as *'the shadow self'*).

> *You cannot meet your spirit without meeting your wounded self.*

Your spirit knows itself to be your wounded self; it is not afraid of this realization in the way that we are in human form. Your excitement to meet your spirit is equally your excitement to meet your shadow self because your excitement —*which is your clearest form of guidance*—is your perception of the experience of your spirit (which acts as an invitation to feel its experience within your mortal self).

Our fear convinces us that we are looking at our wounds in order to heal them, when in fact, the focus of our fear is on a negative, divisive belief about life — a belief that keeps us separate from both the healing of those wounds and the full experience of *all that we are*. Despite how much it may have dominated your life, your wounded self is the part of you that you know the least.

> *Within the integration of all that you have separated off as your pain, wounds, and darkness lies the realization of all that you are.*

WHO CREATED SUFFERING?

"I choose to be conscious of the ways in which my relationship with suffering is shaping my life."

Our relationship with the perception of suffering significantly shapes our experience of reality. Suffering is the hardest quality of human existence to not label as being *'a wrongness'* or mistake. Your relationship with it is one that will take time to reorient such that you can experience it in an empowering way.

Accepting the existence of suffering is not to resign yourself to it; it is a realization that seeking to eradicate it only perpetuates its presence.

True freedom from suffering comes from changing your relationship with it through a shift in perception. This is a powerful act of self-empowerment. By acknowledging that suffering is a part of the human experience, and by accepting it, we can learn from it and grow.

Imagining a vantage point from which
suffering is not viewed negatively
but as a transformative act.

To imagine this is a powerful point of inspiration and hope, as it allows us to imagine the state of existence of spirit — the part of us that does not fear suffering.

To know that you created your own suffering, combined with the realization that *'we are one'—which is the experience of your spirit—*is to know at our level of unified consciousness that you are the creator of suffering because you are *the one consciousness/God.*

The transformation of your relationship
with suffering comes from knowing
yourself as its creator.

The final acceptance we grant in our journey to accept *all that we are* is the acceptance of the existence of suffering. Within the knowing of suffering—*because it is the lynchpin of the illusion that we have always resisted—*is *'the knowing of self as as the creator of your experience (God).'* This does not mean that you need to continue to suffer to awaken. It means there is a window through which you can step out of the illusion of individuality, and it looks like the realization that—*as the one consciousness—*you are that which has been every human that has ever existed.

You contain the entire human experience,
from its greatest joy to its greatest suffering.

There is no more you can learn about suffering. The evidence for this is that you are now realizing you are its creator (which is the last thing that can be learned about it).

You cannot know yourself as the creator of
your reality as long as you deny that you
are the creator of all the suffering you have
ever experienced within your reality.

CLARIFICATIONS & REFLECTIONS

We did not become human just so that we could remember our immortality after having made it unconscious (which we have to do to experience mortality). The finite lifespan of our human self always leads us back to the remembering of our spirit when we die.

To remember our immortality prior
to death is called awakening.

Rather than being some idealized goal we created for ourselves to achieve, spiritual awakening is better understood as the journey through a back door—*as opposed to the birth-death front door*—in the illusion that forms the human experience.

To spiritually awaken is to awaken to your spirit. To awaken is for the mortal self to remember that it is immortal. This is to reconnect with the experience of your spirit (which is why awakening is an experience of remembering).

The experience of awakening has infinite faces.

However, because of the trauma of suffering, the final experience within the journey of awakening is met through the part of the self that is most resisted. This is the integration of the unified, collective state of consciousness within us—*the one consciousness*—that knows itself to have experienced all human suffering.

> *To reveal your greatest freedom, you*
> *must reveal your greatest pain; only*
> *by seeing your wounds clearly will you*
> *understand why you created them.*

Suffering is a quality of human life that—*regardless of how much you resist it*—you will always be in a relationship with. How you feel about its existence is a feeling you carry — a feeling that constantly feeds into the creation of your personal reality.

Although there is nothing wrong in raging at suffering or feeling depressed about it, it is important to understand that these fear-based emotions can only ever increase the presence of suffering in your life. Indeed, they are a significant part of the face of your suffering because...

> *...to resist your experience is to suffer.*

How you feel about your suffering is the part of your relationship with it that you can best transform through your point of choice in the present moment. By consciously choosing to look at *'Why I have created the suffering in my life?'* instead of viewing it as a mistake, you empower yourself to no longer play the role of victim in relation to the wounds you have yet to resolve. This is an unfolding journey that takes time. Do not repress your feelings of anger, anxiety, or depression through an idea they are to be resisted.

> *Only in meeting your pain can you*
> *understand why you chose it.*

THE FEAR OF FREEDOM

*"I choose to realize the ways in
which I fear my own being."*

As wonderful as the limitless potential of freedom sounds, there are ways in which you fear it. Realize the perspective from which it can be said that you must fear the freedom of your spirit, or you would be living it. You will know when you are in the state of freedom consciousness because, in that timeless moment, you will be living your dream.

Freedom consciousness is a state of mind where you are aware of and embrace the limitless potential of freedom; as wonderful as this sounds, it is frightening to that which is accustomed to being limited. To be in a state of limitlessness is to be in a state of infinite possibility. This is a state where anything can potentially happen.

*The unconstrained possibility of
complete change—the antithesis of*

consistency—is a fundamental root
fear within the human experience.

When we are in fear, we resist states of change because
we do not feel we can control or predict the outcome. As
you awaken into freedom consciousness, you will face any
internalized fear-based inclinations or attachments to reality
being *consistent/unchanging.* In this, realize how the need for
consistency points to the wider nature of fear and is the main
reason we fear the state of fear itself (regardless of what it is
focused on).

To fear something is to give it energy,
and to give something energy is to
fuel its state of manifestation.

This is the process through which we tend to create what we
fear. Therefore, in a state of freedom consciousness, where
all is instantaneously possible, our fear instantly begins to
manifest. Your consciousness knows this, and as long as it
knows itself to contain fear, it will fear freedom because to
enter freedom is to face that fear.

In the state of freedom consciousness, to face and feel your
fear is to live in the manifestation of that fear — just as to be
in joy is to instantly be in an expression of bliss. To be within
the infinite potential of freedom, you cannot fear your mortal
self or your spirit. To enter the state of fear is to exit the state
of freedom.

In the mortal state, we each play with the
juxtaposition of fear and freedom.

When our fear of freedom is seen clearly, the reasons why
people choose limitation over freedom become clear. To

release your limitations is to release your fears, which can only be done by facing them. It is to make conscious what you have feared being conscious.

Your fears are your limitations.

By facing and transforming your fears through your willingness to be changed, you will enter the awakened state, which is to say, the free experience of *all that you are.*

Do not seek to eradice fear; instead, transform it into a catalyst for growth and self-discovery.

CLARIFICATIONS & REFLECTIONS
The idea that we could fear freedom may initially sound illogical because of how we are naturally drawn to things that feel good and resist things that feel bad. Becoming conscious of the ways in which you fear freedom allows you to see through the romanticized version of it. This understanding reveals the intricate relationship between fear and freedom.

> Freedom is not the opposite of slavery because freedom includes the freedom of consciousness to experience being a slave.

> Freedom is the allowance of all.

> Freedom is freedom from fear.

> Freedom is to allow yourself to be conscious of all *things/states/qualities.*

> Freedom is unconditional and equal love for all.

> Freedom loves and allows slavery as much as it loves and allows liberation.

Freedom loves and allows starvation as much as it loves and allows obesity.

Freedom loves and allows suffering as much as it loves and allows bliss.

Freedom loves and allows separation through fear as much as it loves and allows unity through love.

This realization of freedom is particularly challenging for those seeking to create themselves through the attempted replication of a mental ideal rather than from what they feel themselves to be. In this state, *'being free'* is a significant part of the aspirational ideal, and the person will only accept positive, feel-good descriptions of what freedom is. Freedom is, therefore, seen as a state of entirely positive bliss, instead of a state of love and allowance for all things (which embraces both positive and negative).

When someone says they want to be free, they usually mean they want to be in bliss. Although these statements are technically the same—*as to be free is to blissfully live your dream*—what their concept of bliss does not contain is the understanding that the bliss of being in freedom arises by entering the allowance of freedom — the kind of freedom through which you allow yourself to meet all you have resisted meeting through fear (which is to integrate all you have previously repressed).

The clearer intent is to desire the bliss that arises through the allowance of 'all that you are' to freely be as it is — even if that means losing control to face the fears within you.

NO RULES

"I choose to experience all perceived rules as personal choices in the moment— and not as eternal universal laws."

T he physical laws which appear to govern your existence do not define you — you define them. Scientists seek to study and reveal the physical laws that underlie the natural world. They seek to uncover how physical reality came to be. In this, they typically believe religion does not contain any truth that would be meaningful in this endeavor.

Scientists seek to demonstrate how the *'divine order'* within the universe is purely mathematical and logical in nature, as they do not believe consciousness could have played any role (due to their belief that consciousness did not exist when the physical universe came into being).

What scientists may not fully realize is that they are not just discovering physical

*laws but also creating and shaping
them through their consciousness.*

Scientists, through their beliefs and the choices they make
in creating their measuring devices, influence the results of
their experiments. This is demonstrated in the double-slit
experiment, where the act of observation affects the behavior
of light, causing it to behave either as a particle or a wave.
They will always find more of what they are looking for —
unfolding it into every *greater/finer* detail.

*Reality is a unique projection created
by each of us. There is no right or
wrong to how you experience it.*

The methods of the scientist are as valid as that of the overtly
spiritual. We each contain *all that reality is* and have the ability
to intersect our personal realities to create a seamless mass
reality. *All that you are* is encoded into your reality, and the
scientist is exploring not only *what reality is* but also *what they
are* through the external manifestation of reality.

*The scientist seeks to answer the same
primal question as the spiritual explorer.*

We are all on the journey of 'know thyself.'

You are not here to discover who you are, as if it were written
on some tablet in heaven with you here on a spiritual quest to
reveal it. Just like the scientist, *you are creating who you are.*

What you are is what you choose to be, and in exploring
states of being, you further refine what it is you are choosing
to be. Realize this, and you will begin to grasp how exciting
your freedom is. There are no permanent rules. You are the

architect of your own identity, free to explore and refine it as you wish.

You are making all the rules
up as you go along.

This realization may seem daunting, but it also empowers you to take control of your life and shape it according to your heart.

You are the creator of your
mortal self—not the discoverer
of what you already are.

Face your fears of the enormity
of this realization.

CLARIFICATIONS & REFLECTIONS

To say that scientists are creating the physical laws of the universe as they discover them is not to imply they are retroactively changing physical history. It is equivalent to the advances in our understanding of consciousness changing not only our mental understanding of ourselves but also how we experience ourselves to be at a feeling level. For example, the Christian Bible has impacted not only what we mentally conceive being human to be but also how we feel about ourselves.

How religious concepts are worded is significant and can alter our path of evolution. Religion's view of sin gives a misleading idea of why we carry feelings of unworthiness, shame, and guilt. In defining the word *'sin,'* the author created *the idea of sin* within the consciousness of humanity.

Whether or not you identify as religious,
the concept of sin has affected you, as even
to reject it as truth is still to have had a
relationship with it as a possibility.

At this point in history, the laws that science is simultaneously creating and describing through observation are predominantly in the territory of quantum physics. As scientific instruments become more capable of detecting ever smaller particles, scientists are entering a level of reality that humanity has not previously been present at (in terms of awareness). In describing what these particles are—*and their potential effects in better understanding the origins of the universe*—science is engaging in a process that is, at its core, no different from labeling certain feelings as being connected to the idea of sin.

Both science and religion shape how
human reality is not only interpreted/
understood but how it feels to exist in.

Our language can only ever point to the existence of something. Words alone cannot contain, absolutely define, or completely describe anything. This realization that '*the language is not the reality*' is commonly expressed as '*the map is not the territory.*'

Your understanding of yourself is not what you are — it is only ever the best attempt of your embodied self to describe not only the nature of itself but the nature of *the one consciousness/ All That Is.*

SELF-DETERMINATION

*"I choose to determine my reality
with love and joy."*

When seen from the wider perspective of your spirit, the discovery of the human self is the creation of the human self. This can also be expressed as ... through the creation of a human self—*which is inherently reflective*—spirit discovers a new perspective of itself and thereby enhances its knowing of itself.

To embrace this realization, make room in your life to both discover *what you already are* and create *what you are becoming.* As much as you are here to discover a new perspective on yourself, it is also true to say you are here to determine yourself through your human experience of will. There is no right or wrong in what you create yourself to be — for there is only being. Do not fear directly *knowing/seeing* that you are the one determining yourself.

> *Realizing that you are self-determined is not just a concept; it's a catalyst for positive action.*

Just as significant is how the realization of self-determination is an invitation to let go of the fear-based belief that some opposing force is working against you. When there is no longer an opponent—*which you may have defined as evil, greed, selfishness, lust, inauthenticity, or temptation*—then there is no longer a need to try to control your own creation from a place of anxiety, fear, or a belief that you can go wrong.

Self-determination is the sovereign realization that the invisible, guiding force you feel behind your life is you. To know you are self-determined is to feel yourself as present in what would have previously been perceived as *'being divine.'* It is to see your hand in every miracle that you experience. It is to know that fully being yourself is the source of joy.

> *To feel self-determined is to stand in your power.*

To stand in your power is to recognize yourself as the ultimate determinant in your personal reality. Your freedom to shape your reality is yours alone, a testament to the design of this reality. This is not to say that your mortal self is the most powerful force in *the* universe — it is to say that you are the most powerful force in *your* universe.

> *You are the determinant of your reality.*

> *Determine your reality with love and joy, and you will live in love and joy.*

> *Determine your reality with fear, lack, and suffering, and you will live in fear, lack, and suffering.*

The source of your determination
is your feeling for life.

Determine what you want to feel and open yourself to see any choices you are making that do not align with this desire. Only you can transform your reality into one of love, acceptance, joy, through the allowance of *all that there is* (which is *all that you are).*

CLARIFICATIONS & REFLECTIONS
There are many ways in which the primal question within us can be approached — whether that be:

> *'Who am I?'*
>
> *'What is this?'*
>
> *'Where do I come from?'*
>
> *'Where did this all begin?'*
>
> *'Is there more than what I perceive through my biological senses?'*

Because of its concern with what is currently present, *'Who am I?'* tends to be the most approachable and often becomes a central focus for those on the spiritual path. While it is a powerful question worthy of attention, it carries the presumption that what you are—*despite your ever-changing face*—carries within it some transcendent level of definition that can be accurately described when the correct knowledge is discovered (which you may regard as *'the Truth of you').*

In this is the seeking of 'I am this
— not that' when the deepest
truth is you are all things.

This realization that you are connected to all things does not subsume the value of each of the infinite experiences of connection that can be had with each and every individual.

As you step into the realization that you are the creator of your reality, the question, 'Who am I?' becomes, 'Who do I want to be?'

This shift is not just a change in perspective but a powerful act of self-empowerment. In this, you will notice a shift from wondering about your spiritual heritage—*which you will fully remember upon death*—to fantasizing about who you can be and what you can do in this present lifetime.

It is disempowering to your present self to predominantly focus your spiritual journey on the past and future — the remembering of and returning to your spiritual heritage rather than on the present moment. When your mortal self dies—*and returns to the knowing of its infinite nature*—what will be most exciting is not the return to that which you have eternally known and been, but the full knowing and assimilation of the mortal life you are currently present within.

Seek to discover yourself through the creation of yourself in this lifetime.

Seek to unashamedly be yourself — both inwardly and outwardly.

You will find that you make the most profound discoveries about yourself and the nature of reality by *expressively/ creatively* being yourself, rather than by thinking about 'Who am I?'

THE MEANING OF IMPERFECTION

"I choose to assign meanings to reality that are empowering, inclusive, and cooperative beccause these qualities best reflect my dream of being."

T he negative conception of imperfection and the state of freedom consciousness are incompatible. Imperfection does not limit you. Imperfection is a fundamental building block of freedom, and that is to say, 'choice.'

Embracing imperfection is a powerful declaration of your freedom.

One of the central paradoxes of human existence is that you are being asked to simultaneously realize that:

You are both perfect and imperfect.

You are infinite, yet limited.

You are eternally immortal, yet know yourself as mortal.

You are God and you are human.

Accept the enormity of the realization that you have created yourself to be free to be all things. The key to directly experiencing this is through the acceptance of the ways in which you believe you are imperfect. This is the side of yourself that is resisted as being *'not ideal.'*

Do not spend your life pursuing a mental definition of perfection; that practice is a denial that you are already perfect. The choice of your spirit to create your mortal self *exactly as it is—including whatever you judge to be your imperfections—*was and is perfect.

> *To accept an imperfection is to stop perceiving it as imperfect.*
>
> *Through acceptance, imperfections are seen to be the 'perfect' idiosyncrasies through which to experience your intention for life.*

What you perceive as imperfect is only imperfect because that imperfection perfectly reflects your belief that you are imperfect. It is a reflection of your own self-judgment. Conversely, whatever you perceive as perfect is experienced as perfect, and your interaction with it will be felt as perfection.

Even while you are trapped within limited beliefs as to what you can affect and change in your life, you are not limited in how you choose to perceive yourself.

Are you a hero or a coward?

Are you a kind person?

Are people fortunate to have you in their life?

Do you make smart choice?

You have the power to either empower or disempower yourself through your choice of perception. This is not suggesting you live your life in an egoic fantasy; it is not about disengaging from the perception of the consensus reality. What changes is the meaning that you assign to what you perceive? The choice of how you perceive yourself is a choice to live within the feeling of either a blessed or cursed life.

> *As much as you derive meaning from reality,*
> *you equally assign meaning to it.*

CLARIFICATIONS & REFLECTIONS

The consensus view of reality can be so strong that it seems like fact; however, no meaning is implicit. Mass socialization is the dominant power in how we assign meaning to reality. Its pervasiveness creates a mass reality through a shared experience of meaning. Beyond the power of this intention to live within a shared world, your reality does not have a predetermined meaning.

> *You can transform any aspect of*
> *your life by changing the meanings*
> *you assign to your experience.*

Because reality is a time-space mirror that reflects us to ourselves—*directly and without distortion*—it is inherently neutral. Reality does not have an agenda for us to have either a positive or negative experience — its neutrality tells us that our experiences are not predetermined to be positive or negative. *'The agenda of reality'* only exists as a reflection of our own agenda to better *'know thyself'* by experiencing what we are when directly reflected as a mortal self within a time-space mirror.

Because we live within not only the mental conception of meaning but also within how that meaning feels, the desire to know ourselves better is not rooted in some desire for difficult or intensely contrasting experiences.

Our desire comes from our love of life.

In religious terms, the reflection of reality is *'the love of God.'* Its neutrality is not a reflection of indifference but our unified desire to be completely free within our experience.

For reality to have an agenda would be to live within a state of being controlled and not to live within either love or freedom. We designed the human experience to express the freedom of our mortal self — not to be controlling of it.

Our desire to be free is an expression of our love for the knowing of self through infinite form.

When you feel like the universe is not supporting you in your endeavors, realize that in showing you to yourself, reality is offering you the deepest and most empowering level of support possible.

Choose to meet reality as an enlightening encapsulation of the love of the one self for your human self. Receive its message as coming from nothing but love.

ALLOW YOURSELF TO FEEL EVERYTHING

"I choose to embrace the infinite realization that I can be anything."

To truly know something is to feel its state of beingness (which is to know what it is to be it). It is the realization of knowing into being through the power of your focus and intention. An empath can experience the *state/feeling* of beingness of whoever they focus on.

Compassion is the ability to unify your perception with others and enter a state of empathy with them.

To be an empath is to exercise your power of reality creation. It is—*for the duration of your focus*—to create the reality of another within yourself. To truly empathize with someone is to know what it is to be them, and that is to be what they are in the moment. It is to travel back to the infinite state of *unity/*

connection through the undoing of all choice and then choose to be that which you wish to empathize with — such that you experience unity with them.

As you trust in yourself and your ability to transform your inner reality in this way, you will be able to experience anything from within its own being. In the moment of doing this, you will directly experience the paradox of being yourself and yet, being able to be all things. There is no experience of being denied to you by anything other than yourself.

There is no thing that you cannot be.

You are free — you are free
to be anything.

To realize you can be anything is to start to become conscious of the wider nature of your beingness that exists beyond the human self you are currently identified with. The more deeply you allow yourself to empathize, the more you will realize that just as you can be anything, it is also true to say that no particular thing can be said to be you.

You are no particular 'thing,' and yet you
have the potential to be any 'thing.'

Recognize yourself as being that which
chooses from a point of infinite choice.

Beyond living in the experience of your choices is the experience of yourself as the creator of those choices — the choices that, when fully contained within human form, we previously viewed ourselves as a result of.

Travel into the heart of your awareness and allow yourself to consciously experience the point of choice — the state of existence from which you choose. Go there. Be there. Know the self that creates your human choices to know your spirit.

You are that which chooses from
within your own choice to be.

CLARIFICATIONS & REFLECTIONS

Beliefs tend to vary as to whether people are innately empathetic and altruistic (a perspective birthed through a belief in our inherent state of connection) or are innately insensitive and selfish (a belief that nothing connects us beyond genetics and our self-centered desire to survive).

Empathy is usually perceived to be a skill in that is seen as a quality we each have to varying degrees that can be improved if we choose to focus on it. Although it is possible to learn how to better see things from the perspectives of others, in seeking to be more empathetic toward others, you are not learning a mental skill — you are seeking to access an aspect of the reality of your spirit. As such, empathy is not a skill you must learn (although mental techniques can be helpful).

Empathy is the state of having
an open-flowing heart.

To feel without restriction
is to be empathetic.

There is no difference between saying *'I am feeling'* and *'I am feeling empathetic.'* All feelings are empathetic of something (most typically your mortal self). This is the realization that just as you may—*through empathy*—experience the beingness within another person, so it is that you are just such a state of empathy held within the perception of your spirit.

To say empathy is the state of feeling
itself is to say that empathy is love.

You cannot truly empathize with others if you cannot love yourself. All feeling that is free of fear is love. Just as you cannot learn to love, you cannot learn to be empathetic. To come to a place of love and empathy is to resolve your fear (which is to allow yourself to experience your intention to be *all that you are*).

Empathy is not a feeling you need to generate — it is the inherent state of feeling that arises when you perceive something without fear or judgment.

To not empathize with someone is
to be in judgment of them.

Despite what we tell ourselves, we are not indifferent toward anything. In wanting to believe you are indifferent to something, you seek to define yourself as detached from it — a denial of connection. Indifference is not the natural state (with '*natural*' meaning the state that arises when we are not in fear), love and the knowing of connection are.

THAT WHICH CHOOSES

*"I choose to know myself as being
that which chooses."*

Your spirit is free but does not experience what we know as choice—*which is to choose between things*—except for the choice to leave the state of infinite consciousness in order to experience choice at the individuated level (the choice to be mortal). We each represent our spirit's choice to experience choice.

*We are the embodied of choice, which is to
say, we are the embodied of freedom.*

Choosing is an act of differentiation. Through the expression of preference, we further define what we are. Your self-definition is a choice you are making in each and every moment. This act of choice does not inherently create limitation; it is that '*to choose*' you must be within an experience of limitation. Within the state of spirit, there is no need to choose between things as all is present).

To choose, you must be within that which can be differentiated into a choice.

You must leave the experience of unity—*inherent to your spirit*—and enter the diversity of embodiment to experience choice.

We are each *'that which chooses.'*

Through your spirit choosing to be what you are, you are the embodiment of the act of choice.

You are the choice of yourself — who you are is who you choose to be.

You are a product of all the choices you have ever made, and yet, you cannot be said to be any particular choice (because there is no choice that you cannot choose to change your perception of).

> *In each moment, you choose yourself anew.*

The original idea for choice was the first choice — it was the creation of choice through the choosing of choice. *Choice chose itself to exist.* You are the choice to choose from within human form.

Within *the one consciousness,* the idea of differentiation and choice *birthed as one.* It is not that the creation of differentiation *then* created the possibility of choice (just like it is not that the realization of choice created the possibility to divide what had previously been unified).

In trying to grasp the idea that diversity and choice birthed simultaneously—*like two sides of the same coin*—it can be seen how predisposed the human mind is to interpret reality as a linear chain of cause and effect. This mental agenda—*to assign the meaning inherent in sequence*—shows how the mind creates the meaning that forms our experience of linear time.

Having left the wider reality to experience the freedom of choice, we naturally desire to recreate the harmony of being within a unified state of consciousness while also maintaining the experience of choice.

> *All hearts are unified in the desire to know*
> *bliss as it is at the heart of what we are.*

CLARIFICATIONS & REFLECTIONS

Through the power of choice, you can focus on whatever qualities of existence you wish. A fundamental quality of our embodiment is the polarity between feeling unified with what surrounds you and feeling *separate/disconnected.*

For those who struggle with life, it is easy to believe that feeling alienated is inherent to being human. But it is the polarity of *unified-to-separate* that is inherent — not just the end of the polarity where you feel alone.

> *If you feel isolated, lonely, or alienated,*
> *this is not what you are; it is what you are*
> *choosing to experience in this moment.*

Just as you have chosen the states of perception that have led you to conclude that life is inherently lonely, you also have the power to choose the states of perception that will lead you to feel connected. This is not to imply that you are *'to blame'* for your negative experiences (which is a fear-based interpretation). It is to understand that your most difficult experiences are what you—*from the level of your spirit*—wanted to experience.

It is impossible for past choices to be a mistake, even if they led you to have a painful experience. Any idea to the contrary comes from your lack of understanding about your *wider nature/infinite nature/origin/intentions for this life.*

> *Through your choices, you have the power to both unify and divide.*

The key to freedom within the human experience is the state of Unified Diversity (which is to create the experience of unity through honoring all diversity). To accept diversity in yourself is to allow freedom for both yourself and others.

Whether conscious of it or not, at the deepest level, every human seeks the experience of Unified Diversity. We each wish to know ourselves as completely as possible, and that must include the nature of our unity as well as our diverse and uniquely individualized qualities.

> *By seeing your choices as acts of self-creation—rather than a by-product of life—you will bring far more conscious awareness to each choice you make.*

This is to no longer *'step over'* your choices as if they were not choices at all. This is to open your eyes to see just how many choices you may be making on auto-pilot (which is to act as if you had no other real options). This empowering step will further engage you with reality as you will have a much more direct experience of how it is that you are *creating/steering* your life.

BE BOLD = BE SOMETHING NEW = BE YOURSELF

"I choose to open myself to new and exciting experiences of self."

Y ou both are your spirit and are not your spirit. Imagine your spirit as an expression of all possibility. In human form, we are not all possibility in that we are a chosen focus of self, but that focus of a human self is created from the state of all possibility. Moreover, the potential for all possibility continues to exist within us but in an encoded form (meaning physicality, reality, and our embodied self are each expressions of the state of *all possibility/infinity*).

As you explore and develop the expression of yourself, so you decode your chosen focus within *all possibility* into all that you choose to express yourself to be in each moment. All that you perceive—*which is an expression of all possibility, regardless of whether you perceive it as external or internal*—is like a menu that aids you in your *selection/creation* of your mortal self.

> *Imagine your spirit as an open rose.*

You are the seed of that rose. You contain the complete awareness to transform yourself into the rose. There are infinite ways in which you can do this — ways which, in this moment, you are creating with your freedom of perception. As you discover new and exciting ways of becoming the rose, so you enhance the rose — you enhance *the one consciousness*.

You are *the one self/the one consciousness* in a state of expressing and exploring the freedom of consciousness to be. To be in a state of freedom is not the same as being all that *the one consciousness* is, yet there is no state within *the one consciousness* that you are not free to explore.

> *There is nothing you cannot be and*
> *no quality you cannot embody.*
>
> *Your choice is unlimited.*
>
> *Your potential is infinite.*

This is how you are simultaneously limited and unlimited — singular, yet infinite.

This is how you both are and are not your spirit.

This is how your spirit both is and is not *the one consciousness*.

This is how you are.

This is what allows you to be in the experience of an individuated self.

To see this is to realize why you should not *seek to be all* — you should seek to be yourself. *The All* already exists as *All That Is/ the one self.* You, however, are the only state of being that exists as you.

> *You are unique in your expression*
> *of the one consciousness.*

Your potential is that of a birthing God in human form. Do not destroy yourself to become what already exists.

> *Be bold, be what you came to be, and*
> *that is to say, 'be something new.'*

CLARIFICATIONS & REFLECTIONS

One of the hardest concepts to grasp about your spirit is the different ways in which you can perceive it. You can do this both as your personal spirit (which creates a possessive feeling) and as *the one consciousness* (which creates a non-possessive feeling). With both ways of perceiving your spirit being valuable in understanding consciousness, this can initially be seen as a paradox, but both vantage points are necessary to comprehend your infinite nature.

One technique to see how something paradoxical can be contained within something singular is to imagine it like a swimming pool that goes from shallow to deep. The pool, like your spirit, cannot be said to be shallow or deep as it contains both opposing qualities. Yet, just as you can choose to focus your perception on one quality over the other in the pool, you can also choose to perceive your spirit from a personal or non-possessive perspective.

Applying this technique to the perception of your spirit is to see it as being like the swimming pool, but with one end strongly focused on you (that feels to be your personal spirit and reflects your own singular concern for your embodied self). The other end is focused on the big picture (which feels to be connected to everything in existence in an impartial way). So the shallow end would be seen as *'your spirit,'* and the deep end would be seen as *'the collective of all spirit'*/All That Is/ *the one consciousness*.

> *You might be tempted to see the two ends of the pool/spirit as separate entities, but they are not.*

Every human being has their own unique shallow end (their personal spirit), each like a facet of a single diamond *(the one consciousness/God)*. Just as you cannot detach a facet of a diamond from that diamond, you cannot detach your personal experience of spirit from the entirety of what *spirit/ the one consciousness* is.

> *We are all interconnected, each a unique part of the whole.*

Your spirit is initially best met through a *personalized/ possessive* state of perception, as this is closest to your current experience of self. As you further grasp, embrace, and embody all that the infinite is, you will travel into the depths of your spirit by discovering how your embodied self is connected to everything through it. Every individual is a facet of the diamond and cannot be separated from the whole.

> *You contain the ability to perceive at the level of the whole, the facet, and everything in between.*

THE CHOICE OF YOURSELF

*"I choose to be the conscious
choice-maker in my life."*

Human individuality—*which is formed through the differentiation of time and space*—is an evolving experience (due to it being a translation of self over linear time). Being *the one consciousness* in human form, you are the experience of yourself. You *seek/unfold* experience by following the guiding impulses of your heart—*which naturally arise within an experience of differentiation*—to explore the aspects of the diversity that most excite you in this world.

*You exist within the experience
of your beliefs.*

The reality you experience flows out from the meanings you ascribe to the collective of everything you believe. Regardless of how it may sometimes seem, you are the one who chooses what you believe.

> *The responsibility for your beliefs*
> *is ultimately your own.*

In each moment, you can choose to believe something new. In each moment, you are *re-choosing/reaffirming* every belief that you do not change. Do not give the power of the choice of your beliefs to any other person, as that is to give them the power to choose your experience of reality for you (until you choose to take that power back).

> *Even if you give your power away to the*
> *greatest degree possible, the choice to take*
> *back that power is always with you.*

The freedom of your will is your freedom to experience and explore diversity. You chose this life to experience infinite choice. It is up to you to use that freedom within the living of this life. No one else can make you *'be free.'* If you do not use your power of choice—*which is not wrong or a mistake*—you will automatically choose from the collective, mass beliefs about reality you have subconsciously absorbed from society.

To be empowered in your freedom is to be aware of your choices such that you can choose consciously from a state of awareness — rather than unconsciously from the fear-based beliefs you have assimilated.

> *Elevate yourself to the position where*
> *you know you are the only one who can*
> *step forward to choose for yourself.*

Choose from your experience of self, your feeling, your resonance, your joy, and your excitement (rather than from the mass belief). When you choose with love, you put that love into the mass belief system that affects *all who choose to not choose* by default.

> *To choose love for yourself is to make
> the whole world more love-based.*

CLARIFICATIONS & REFLECTIONS

If you are not willing to make choices in your life, others will make your choices for you. This occurs by default whenever you disregard your power of choice. This effect can be direct, through a person you have given your power (whether through fear or the belief they are superior and will make better choices). It can also be indirect, through your unquestioned beliefs.

The human experience has a mass belief system—*passed on through socialization*—that has developed in a fear-based direction. This has led it to be based in the principles of separation, disconnection, hierarchy, competition, and survival of the fittest. Because fears are based on unconsciousness, we tend to align with the mass thinking about whatever we fear.

When you disregard your power to consciously hoose as the individual you want to be, instead of owning your individuality and its potential for freedom, you take your choice of experience from the mass without thought or question. It is to follow the mass (rather than stand in your power and lead yourself).

> *It is not wrong to be a follower for a period
> for of time, but eventually you must take the
> steering wheel of your life to create all the
> diverse qualities of your unique dream.*

Choosing from the mass belief does not lead to the complete homogenization of choice because it occurs with degrees of localization. The beliefs of people close to you and the ideological groups you belong to have a greater effect on you than those with whom you have a more distant association.

This occurs at a subconscious level — meaning the mass beliefs can affect your choices without that effect being perceived. When this happens, the person does not realize they are giving away their power of choice as they are still technically choosing from their own beliefs. It is just that their own belief on the matter was assimilated—*either passively or fearfully*—and is, therefore, an unexplored mass belief.

The same idea of personal versus mass beliefs applies to following your heart (rather than the crowd). Sometimes it feels good to go with the flow and be a part of a unified crowd. There are also times when you may feel caught in the flow of people around you in a way that is not enjoyable. Learn to differentiate between the two, such that when you are not enjoying where the mass flow is taking you, you can simply— *and without drama*—excuse yourself and do something that feels more joyful.

Do not be afraid to wield your power of choice.

LIMITATION & LIMITLESSNESS

*"I choose to know myself as a perfect
expression of limitlessness."*

T he purpose of this reality is to create and be. If you feel
there must be a positive direction, call it *'coming to
freedom through the allowance and following of your
feelings,'* which, practically speaking, means not choosing
from fear-based limited beliefs. Choosing the path of freedom
from fear is to enter the state of consciousness, which is in
allowance of *all that you are.*

*The mind is not an enemy that your
heart is standing in opposition to.*

Just because choosing from your feelings—*rather than your
mind*—will lead you to experience yourself in freedom, it does
not then follow that experiencing ourselves in limitation is
'wrong' or *'bad.'*

At this time of awakening, when we want to see through the illusion of separation—*rather than go further into it*—following our hearts over our minds aligns with this intention. This world—*and who we experience ourselves to be in it*—has only been possible because we had minds with which to create and evolve such incredible contrast and diversity. In the early stages of the human experience, we wanted to focus on the concepts of separation that arose within our minds.

> *Even though the mind is no longer the compass to follow, our thoughts are still of great value and intrigue.*

You became human to realize and express *all that you are.* The reward is the realization of the joy you have encoded in your human form (which is unlocked through following your *heart/inner feeling of guidance*). This evolving joy-based journey is experienced in a unique and powerful way when realized from within a reality defined by limitation.

A part of being human—*a form limited in its perception by design*—is appreciating how its limitations create a powerful vantage point from which the self can better comprehend the nature of both joy and freedom. Even in limitation, you are a perfect expression of freedom. This is the paradox of how limitation can evolve the experience of freedom. By understanding and accepting our limitations, we can gain a unique perspective that allows us to fully appreciate the joy and freedom that exist within and beyond those limitations.

> *With this realization, a person is no longer contained by the polarity of freedom versus limitation.*

This is awakening, and it is to step into a new dimension of being that is—*from our current perspective*—best described as freedom within limitation. This state of being, also known as the state of Unified Diversity, is a condition where one is free to be oneself within the limitations of the human form while also acknowledging and appreciating the diverse expressions of others.

CLARIFICATIONS & REFLECTIONS

The heart is an emotion-based guidance system. When we act from fear and create a reality that we feel resistant to—*a feeling we interpret as negative*—that resistance is felt to be in opposition to something we do our best to mentally identify and name. A negative feeling conveys that you are operating from a position of fear. It is not saying that whatever you have mentally identified as the focus of your resistance is *'wrong,'* *'bad,'* or *'needs to be extinguished.'* This is rarely how it is understood because, as a species, we have become predisposed to labeling and segregating everything (instead of seeing it as a unified reflection).

Another common misunderstanding is that a negative feeling around the idea of doing something does not mean it will *never* be enjoyable. It means it is not the most enjoyable thing to do *at that particular moment*. Therefore, if you do not label the idea itself as *'bad,'* the next day, you may have a positive feeling about the same idea — indicating that the present moment is a better time to act on the idea.

To a degree, the interpretation of feelings as being for the purpose of placing value-judgment labels on external things (versus the interpretation of feelings as guiding us in the moment without the notion of judgment) is what led to the idea of *'good'* standing in opposition to *'bad.'* This mentally evolved into *right versus wrong* (and, by extension, *good versus evil)*, further entrenching the idea of life being a struggle against something.

This marked our shift from choosing from a personal feeling of preference in the heart to deciding what is the *'right'* versus *'wrong'* thing to do from a mental belief that certain things —*whether people, feelings, thoughts, or choices*—are inherently and universally either *'right or wrong.'*

What was developed as a mental tool to aid our understanding of the process of choosing from the heart became a tool of control that takes power by promoting the fear of doing the *'wrong thing'* and being labeled as *'bad'* or *'evil.'*

THE ALL

*"I choose to experience my choices
as being perfect for all."*

Our collective dream of freedom can only come to be through each individual living their personal dream because that is the shared path. This is the case no matter what your dream is — even if, on the surface, it appears to be at odds with the collective. Your dream fits perfectly into the collective dream because it—*just like you*—is not separate.

As you live your dream, you will start to see its part in the overall harmony and motion of *'the All.'* You are in harmony with *'the All'* — whether you perceive it or not. Even those who appear to be purely of service to themselves are being of service to *'the All.'* The distinction of *service-to-self* versus *service-to-others* is an illusion (because self and others are only perceptually separate within illusion).

All service is service to 'the All.'

All action is action for 'the All.'

All love is love for 'the All.'

All hate is hate for 'the All.'

Everything is for 'the All.'

You are free to act, think, and feel in any direction. To know this is to be free from fear because all action that flows from your loving heart—*rather than the fears within your mind*—is seen to be *'right action.'* All action is valuable because all action is a mirror. All action is perfect — because even imperfections are perfect.

The choices present in your life
do not exist to test you.

Your self-created choices are part of the game of life and represent access to different *versions of reality/timelines* available for you to select (according to what your belief system will allow). The feeling of choices being a test is not because *'that is how reality is'* — it is a direct result of our mental attachments to achieving a particular destination.

The more attached you are to experiencing something *in particular,* the more your choices will appear to lead you in *'the right'* or *'the wrong'* direction. If you are attached to a specific outcome, you will not experience freedom in your choices. Embrace the freedom in your choices, and—*even if you are not yet ready to act*—know that as *'right action'* also.

You are free to choose as you wish, and
whatever you decide will be perfect for
'the All' and not just for yourself.

Your deepest desires stem from the desire for freedom and the root of all your fears is the fear of freedom. In freedom, there is no plan, no God to rule over you, no necessity for consistency, and no direction that is best to follow. There is only your will, and from your will, you create all that you experience. Trust yourself to give yourself love, and all will be loved by that love.

Trust your heart, and all will be freer
as a result of your freedom.

CLARIFICATIONS & REFLECTIONS

Letting go of the idea that certain directions are wrong is challenging as your mind can easily conjure unpleasant—*or even horrific*—outcomes to the situations currently unfolding in your life. Logic tells us the only mechanism for control is our ability to make choices. Therefore, we tend to believe these unpleasant scenarios will only happen if we make the '*wrong choice.*'

Thoughts of a negative outcome do not describe an emerging probability you are detecting because you must avoid it (fear-based perception). They are hypothetical mental projections reflecting the fears and judgments currently operating within you.

These thought-forms are not your current reality — your reality is the present moment before you, translated into time and space. However, if you continually focus on your negative thoughts, then, by expressing your freedom to be, those fears will be translated into your present moment (such that you experience reflections of them).

Fear, attachment, and
judgment are connected.

We naturally translate our emotional fears into mental judgments (which are expressed as divisive beliefs). These fear-based beliefs are then experienced as blocks in reality as they describe a territory of being we are resistant to experiencing. This results in the infinite playground of being —*which we each exist within*—to be experienced as a maze (because many paths appear to be blocked). This leads to the feeling—*and therefore the belief*—of '*I am not free*' even though you are in a completely open territory.

> *Resistance is emotional and fluid, but the mental blocks it can create perceptually appear to be solid and impenetrable.*

All the walls in the maze of your life are of your own creation. This is not saying that the walls are '*wrong.*' The mazes that our fear-based walls create are an exquisite creation that represent a dilemma of being created through unconsciousness through which *the one consciousness* is experientially exploring itself.

When you realize that all blocks are mental projections of your fears, the world will no longer feel so inflexible or impenetrable. Whereas previously, you may have been looking for the best way to endure the limitations you face, you will now see how these blocks are clear signposts to fears that still operate within you. This allows you to identify and transform those fears.

> *The mazes we live within describe our fears.*

MEANT

*"I choose to acknowledge myself as the
author of my life script, possessing the
power to change it however I please."*

Discover the infinite freedom that lies in realizing there
is no choice you are *'meant'* to make in a certain way.
There is nothing in your life that you were *meant* to
do — nothing you were predestined to do.

Within the timelessness before birth, there are many things
your spirit imagined it might do in human form, but do not
extrapolate this to conclude that you are *meant* to do these
things. They are simply ideas you felt might be exciting
to explore. You are free to explore them in this lifetime, in
another lifetime, or never; there is no *'meant'* to it — *meant* is a
mental illusion.

If you are insistent on thinking in terms of some *'Master Plan'*
that you are meant to follow, first realize that it can only ever

be your personal Master Plan, and, in each moment, that plan is being adapted through the integration of your mortal experience and you are the one adapting it.

> *To believe in a predestined Master Plan is to not want responsibility for your own choices.*

It is to want to be an actor in a play written by some external force. This is the desire to divorce yourself from the ownership of the feelings of the immediacy, the vibrancy, and the unpredictability of life due to a fear of uncontrollable change.

With the realization that nothing is *'meant'* to happen, there is no loss of purpose or drive (except that which is fear-based). See that any plan you feel inside yourself—*even if it explores something as open as the freedom of all life*—is still *your* plan. And, as the author, you can change it however you desire.

The signature on the intention for your life—*which you may call your blueprint or personal plan*—is that of *the one consciousness,* and as you rewrite it, so you will re-sign it.

> *In this life, you are here to be what you (the you that is present reading these words) want to be.*

If you must think in terms of an external God, then realize the only plan God has for you is to *realize, feel,* and *be* whatever you want to be. As you explore yourself, you will discover your exploration of *all that you are* is *the one consciousness's* exploration of itself. Furthermore, that *'truth'* is no more or no less than *being true to yourself.*

> *If there is a 'Will of God,' then it is for you to experience your own will by using it.*

CLARIFICATIONS & REFLECTIONS

The paradox of how consciousness can be free, yet each mortal life is bound by an *'intention to be in human form,'* is a profound concept that often perplexes those seeking a deeper understanding of reality. This paradox, rooted in the dichotomy of free will and determinism, challenges us to embrace a broader perspective that accommodates both qualities.

One way to think of this is that our intention for this life tends to predetermine a certain emotional territory to be explored, but we are then free in how we explore it. For example, we may choose to explore the experience of addiction, but what form the addiction takes is chosen from within the life. Or we may choose to explore becoming deeply identified with a rigid mindset, but what belief system that will be—*whether religious or scientific*—is chosen from within the life.

With this understanding of our intention for our embodiment, the logical mind can argue that we are not truly free if we are predisposed to explore a certain territory. However, this fails to recognize that the choice for the territory was still made by you—*because you are your spirit*—from within a state of freedom.

> *You chose you own confines.*
>
> *You are your own jailer.*
>
> *You are your own liberator.*

Some argue that we are not free if we are limited in this life by the choices we made before birth (which is perceived as *'in the past'*). However, even though your spirit creates the intention for your embodiment, it is not a choice made *'in the past'* — it is a choice made from *a timeless state*.

While in human form, we perceive *'before our birth'* as the past, but that is an illusion. What we call *'the past'* is *present* to our spirit, and any disparity between its decision and what you believe you would prefer can only ever be caused by perspectives you are unconscious of (which your spirit is aware of).

No matter how much you may rage at the ways in which your life feels negatively predetermined, you are only ever raging from a point of fear-based unconsciousness — rather than from the wider awareness of love and connection. This does not make your feelings invalid or not valuable. It is an invitation to dive deeper into them to reach a wider understanding through which new realization arises.

Even though negative feelings about being predetermined or imprisoned by your circumstances are based on not recognizing that you are choosing your own experience, those feelings are a part of that choice. All feelings are *invited/consented to/self-created/chosen as* a part of the choice to be human.

Notice how your negative feelings propel you to change to better understand your choice of experience.

LOVE IS THE ANSWER

"I choose to experience myself as love."

Love is the answer. If love does not appear to be the answer, then realize that you are misperceiving love. Just as you cannot express freedom in words, so you cannot express love in words. Often, you are left with the realization of *what love is not*, and that realization can ultimately lead you to discover any fear that still exists within you.

All that is not love is fear.

To face your fears is to transform them into love. Know, therefore, that *all is love.* Fear is freedom denied. It is your choice how you perceive love, and that choice is your power to experience joy and freedom. Love is freedom.

To perceive *all as love* is to perceive from a state of freedom consciousness. To perceive from this state of limitlessness is to perceive from a state of knowing infinite freedom (which is to be in a state of unconditional love for all).

*To realize that what you
fundamentally are is love is to
perceive love in all things.*

To perceive yourself as love is to perceive *'the All'* as love, for you are *'the All'* and *'the All'* is love. The inclusivity of this perception opens up a world of freedom and liberation, where love is the guiding force.

You will always see with the eyes through which you choose to look. This is to say that *you will always see what you are looking for* (because what you are looking for is a representation of what you believe).

*Look with eyes of love,
and you will see love.*

Look with judgment, and you will see things you deem to be *'in need'* of your judgment. As you *realize into being* the love inside of you, you will see the love that surrounds you. To see with love is to transform yourself and your reality into your dream. To see love, you must believe in your freedom to love without restriction.

Believe in love. Love is a choice.

You do not have to choose love.

You do not have to choose freedom.

Love cannot prove itself to you.

Freedom does not have a responsibility to break through to you.

Love is not there to save you.

Love cannot save you because there is nothing to be saved from. If you cannot believe that, then know you can save yourself from anything you perceive a need to be saved from simply through being love.

Love is the answer to all things. To realize this is to realize the infinite nature of love. This is to understand its power to transform all states of consciousness that experience themselves through a lens of limitation. To know love is to be unlimited. To know love is to know yourself as *the one consciousness.*

The one consciousness is love. You are '*the love of God'* in human form. To know love, know yourself. To know yourself, love yourself.

Love is the answer.

CLARIFICATIONS & REFLECTIONS

You are love, and love has no limitations. Love with limitations is conditional love. Conditional love will manifest elements of pain as the representation of its limitations.

Unconditional love can only be felt from within the knowing of freedom.

As long as you do not feel free in some way, you will experience that limitation of freedom as a limitation in your ability to love without condition. In this state, your love will be felt as limited because you feel yourself to be limited. Know that you are the one limiting yourself by not knowing yourself as love. To end your pain, come to know the freedom that exists within your perception of its limitation.

Hurt is love distorted into a limited expression.

To feel unconditional love is to feel love in an unlimited way. It is to experience love for all things without differentiation. *To feel unconditional love for another being is to love them without differentiating their being.* It is to love and accept them in their totality … as a whole. Their totality is their unlimited potential to be all — just as it is yours.

To love another in totality is to love yourself in totality. It is to love all in totality. Love others by allowing them to be whatever they choose to be. To further allow love is to remove restrictions from your love. To end your pain, love more — not less. All hurt is unrealized love.

Let go of how you would like love to be. Let go of what you think love should be. Realize how these preconceptions of love often stem from trying to protect and possess your attachments. Release these preconceived notions of what love is, and you will find love in all things.

> *Be willing to see love in all things,*
> *and all you will see is love.*

See with eyes of unconditional love, and you will release any pain you are still carrying. To overcome wounding within you is to transform an obstacle that was stopping you loving others — and that is to transform your pain into love.

Many people think that *'being loving'* is being kind, and, as such, love becomes an act performed. Seek to *'be love.'* This is about how you choose to perceive this world, its inhabitants, and yourself. This is not an abstract feeling. When you see with eyes of unconditional love, you experience yourself as unconditional love — and that is to know you are free and that you exist within an infinite playground.

THE IDEA OF YOURSELF

*"I choose to unleash the power of my
imagination on the creation of my life."*

Your human form is an evolving state of definition
created through a combination of patterns of
identification with and patterns of resistance to *All
That Is/the one consciousness.* It is a medium of separation
that allows infinite consciousness to experience itself
in limitation. This is achieved by your spirit ceasing to
experience itself as everything and instead focusing *an idea
of a self* that is defined within time and space — making it
mortal.

*Your human form is your idea of being
human; you are the idea of yourself.*

*You are the one who is, in each and
every moment, determining what
the idea of yourself is.*

As we are each fundamentally infinite, what comes to most directly define us is not determined by what we will allow, but by what we *resist/separate from/forget.* Although this does technically mean we are limited (which has a negative connotation), the intention for this limitation is to create a positive focus on whatever human experience our spirit desires.

Everything your heart desires potentially exists within the experiential focus of your human life so, in that regard, it is not limiting. Only through self-imposed restrictions—*created through resistance to your human experience*—can you bash your head against reality.

The one consciousness is unlimited. It is on the infinite path of *discovering/experiencing* all the ways in which it is limitless. This is the paradox of how something can be perfect and yet evolving.

> *Embracing the paradox of 'an evolving perfection' opens the door to experiences beyond the mind.*

You are not becoming *all that you are* because you already are *all that you are* (namely, your spirit). You are simply remembering what that is. You are on a journey from limitation to limitlessness, and as you take this journey, you will discover new *ways/perspectives* in which you are free to experience.

> *You are the experience of the self-aware, self-determining belief system that observes you.*

> *Your reaction to your self-observation is one of the primary patterns through which you create.*

Your belief system is an evolving expression of how you are experiencing the freedom of self you have granted yourself. The only limits are what you will and will not allow yourself to believe. Your only limit is your unlimited imagination and your self-belief to manifest whatever it is you can imagine.

You are that which you imagine yourself to be.

You are living in your imagination.

You are living within a dream.

So imagine. Imagine. Imagine.

CLARIFICATIONS & REFLECTIONS

It is only semantics as to whether we describe ourselves in terms of *what we allow* or *what we resist*. The description of one is a description of both (as not to allow is to resist). All dualistic polarities are descriptions of a single quality that exists on a perceptually polarized scale (rather than two opposing qualities).

All dualistic descriptions are relative.

For example, fat and thin are two ends of the polarity of the quality of how we perceive someone's weight — they are not two different qualities. How heavy someone looks is not absolute — it is perceptually determined in relation to those who surround them.

Someone who is not in judgment of a quality can express that quality using terms from either end of its dualistic scale. For example, *'I am that which I allow'* is equivalent to *'I am that which I do not resist.'*

Indifference is often a mask for our more subtle feelings of resistance.

When we try to see dualistic terms as separate, we imagine a middle quality, like *'I am indifferent,'* that we think is neither resistance nor allowance. But in reality, feeling indifferent— *like feeling nothing*—is a contradiction.

> *There is nothing for which*
> *we feel nothing.*

We did not design ourselves to feel indifferent. Spirit does not create us with the intention to feel nothing. All things within the human experience are inherently neutral—*as a reflection of the equality of all*—but all perception is inherently charged because it is in a state of change (because we have chosen to experience linear time).

For example, although it is logically possible to think, *'I am indifferent to my weight,'* we do not walk around feeling *'I am indifferent to my weight.'* Generally, we either feel we would like to be at least a little fatter or thinner, or we divide our body up such that there are *'parts of us'* we feel are too fat or too thin.

> *No particular place on a dualistic scale*
> *can be described as indifference.*

There is only allowance and resistance — what we call *'indifference'* is a state of resistance to the whole. To say you are indifferent to something is to say you are in denial of your resistance to it. When it is not altered by fear-based perception, the default state is allowance because our spirit is always aware of the feeling of connection.

FEEL & KNOW

*"I choose to open myself to fully
experience all that I feel."*

The ideological separation of the heart and mind represents the disconnection of our thoughts from our emotions. However, when we see them as one, we realize the unity of our hearts and minds. This understanding of self is a gift, a realization that unifies our perception of reality and makes us feel integrated and whole. It is to unify your perception of reality. All your senses—*those that are biologically visible and those that are currently hidden*—can be unified into one perceptive sense.

*To exercise your complete, unified sense
of perception is to be an empath.*

To be an empath is to experience whatever you perceive as itself. It is to experience the beingness of whatever you focus your perception on.

The mind does not need to be ruled by logic. Feel what you know. Logic is a tool within being — not a rule for being. It is thought without feeling and can only reinterpret—*through extrapolation*—what you already know. Logic is a powerful tool, but when using it, understand that without feeling, it is a vehicle without fuel.

> *The mind, once integrated with*
> *feeling, offers wisdom.*

To experience wisdom is to feel your knowing and to know your feelings. Let your feelings flow through you without inhibition or self-judgment. If you allow yourself to ask questions *'of'* your feelings, they will teach and guide you, empowering you with self-awareness.

Do not question the validity, value, or *'rightness'* of your feelings — no feeling is *'wrong.'* To do so is an attempt to not feel them. Whenever you try to *think* your feelings—*instead of feeling them*—you are perceiving only a glimmer on the surface of their depth. To accept all your feelings is to liberate yourself.

When you know what you feel, there are no questions you need to ask. This is to mentally step back and allow whatever reality your feelings are steering you towards to manifest. When you know what you feel, your feelings will never lead you astray.

Even if your feelings appear to lead you into difficulty, they did not create that difficulty — the difficulty is an outward representation of unresolved feelings within you that you are finding *'difficult.'* These feelings will be met through the process of resolving what has been manifested as an outward difficulty.

If you allow yourself to be a feeling person, you will always be led to your resistance and mental denials such that they may be resolved. So, even though it may be a difficult experience, it is the desired route (as you are then free of the feeling of difficulty).

Feeling without restriction means to step from the cage of your limited beliefs — even beliefs you would not have previously known were limiting. This liberation is about allowing yourself to fully experience your emotions without judgment or restraint, which can lead to a deeper understanding of yourself and your spiritual journey.

CLARIFICATIONS & REFLECTIONS
The thing that has made the human experience so particular in its extreme expression of diversity is not just its ability for us to feel so deeply but our ability to get lost in our imagination.

> *The imagination is the clearest bridge*
> *between the heart and mind due to*
> *the way it draws from both.*

People who do not utilize their imaginations have the greatest difficulty understanding how the heart and mind—*feeling and thought*—are a polarity of the human self. Fantasize and daydream as you did as a young child to become reacquainted with this aspect of yourself — an aspect that implicitly recognizes your thoughts and feelings to be unified.

To reach the heights of separation we experience—*which creates our depth of individuality*—required us to detach from our feelings and identify with fear-based thoughts. Most people's spiritual path is focused on opening their heart because humanity has become so mental. As we awaken to our wider nature, there is a shift back toward the heart and away from the dominance of the mind.

Many spiritual teachings tend to demonize the mind and idealize the heart. They do this by expressing the merits of the heart—*which we have forgotten*—and the shortcomings of the mind—*which we have denied*—thereby pointing those who are mentally focused—*the majority of people*—in the direction of awakening. Although this does make a person more aware of their feelings, it does so at the expense of further entrenching the idea that thought and feeling are separate.

We do not need to reject, demonize, or denigrate what we are not choosing in order to become less identified with. Instead of believing '*the mind is bad — I must feel more,*' you can believe '*I choose to feel more such that my heart and mind are both in balance and fully operational.*'

Because of the mental demonization that tints most spiritual teachings, once your emotions are flowing, the next challenge is to return to feeling good about your mind (including the unwanted thoughts that sometimes go through it). Feeling good about your mind is not about justifying or accepting every thought, but about acknowledging that your mind, with all its complexities and imperfections, is an integral part of your being.

If you are not feeling good about your thoughts, you are not feeling good about yourself. For those with wounded thinking, one of the heart's greatest challenges is to love the mind because of how we tend to blame it for our perceived failures. It is only through that love that your mind can be at peace.

Love your heart and mind as one.

Love yourself as a whole.

YOUR PAIN IS NOT A MISTAKE
IT IS THE SHIT FROM WHICH THE LOTUS BLOOMS

*"I choose to feel any pain I carry so I may
release the experience of love that it denies me."*

To conditionally love is to contain unexpressed love because you are the love of your spirit, felt without condition or limitation. Through this perspective, see how all pain is love unexpressed.

Pain is the denial of love inside you.

You are not destined to live with any pain unless you choose to. This does not mean pain is wrong or a mistake. It is a choice within the human experience, one that you can change by shifting your focus.

Understanding pain is not about learning how to never feel it again; it is about understanding the reasons you choose to feel it. If you cannot accept that you have created your own painful experiences, then you cannot fully know yourself as the creator any of your experiences.

You can mentally deny you are in pain, but *all that you are* is continually expressed into your reality (because reality is a reflection of you as a whole). Any pain within you is fully expressed in every moment. Experience is infinite and eternal. All denial is finite. You will eventually meet and face all the pain within you.

> *The avoidance of pain can only*
> *ever be temporary.*

Even if a pain is not faced within this particular human life, it will be met at death. You will then choose to create a new human life through which that wounded element can be explored. This is not a curse or the old idea of karma; it is simply to say that experiencing your life as painful shows that some part of the intention that created your life is not yet resolved.

The more you attempt to deny pain within you, the more you push it into alternate routes of manifestation where you can no longer deny it — such as an imbalance within your physical body.

> *To transform your pain, you must feel it.*

To feel pain is to travel into its core, where you will find a wound — a love denied (because it is only through your limitation of *the love that you are* that you can be hurt).

To know unconditional love is to have *released/transformed* your pain. To know pain is to not know an aspect of the love that you are. Unconditional love is universal — it is unrestricted love for all ... love that is equally for all. You are love because your creation *was/is* an act of love. Know in your heart that you are love to become conscious of when you are choosing to experience pain.

Pain is your repression of the love that you are.

If you let yourself know your pain,
you will know yourself as love.

CLARIFICATIONS & REFLECTIONS
Freedom is a state of unconditional love. All that hurts is love distorted into a limited expression. To end the pain you may associate as arising from being in human form is to realize that your human form is not innately painful — even though you are choosing to experience many forms of limitations.

However your pain is manifest, its
form has a purpose/message.

No particular experience of pain is a predetermined part of any human life. However, pain is an aspect of the human experience because of the way in which we use fear to create separation. Fear does not need to be painful, but because of how we designed this reality, it is generally experienced as painful until it is resolved.

Pain is an invitation to change
your experience of self.

This makes the experience of pain an unavoidable part of spiritual awakening; it is an integral part of the full-spectrum human experience. That said, there is no particular manifestation of pain that must be experienced.

If you wish to enter the human experience and follow it through to an awakened state, you will inevitably choose many painful experiences across many lives — and yet, you are completely free in your choice of those lives and you will personally create the forms those painful experiences will take.

> *Pain is not inevitable because no being needs to choose to be human.*
>
> *There are infinite other realities to choose from.*

Within embodiment, we can be highly resistant to the idea that we purposefully choose the form of our pain. Shouting...

> *"I would NEVER choose this!"*

Yet, we readily accept that it is not a mistake for a person to choose to focus on becoming excellent at a physical sport through which they will certainly experience physical pain and often risk permanent debilitating physical damage.

Through our spiritual journey, we typically try to *'become something more'* or *'be someone better.'* This is a manifestation of our desire to become someone who is not in pain because we interpret our pain as a symbol of failure or dysfunction. In no longer trying to be someone else—*someone who does not know pain*—seek to be who you are, having faced and resolved the pain you are carrying.

> *Your pain is not a mistake — it is the shit from which the lotus blooms.*

OPEN YOUR MIND TO NON-PHYSICAL PERCEPTION

"I choose to transform my fears by embracing the unknown."

The seeming continuity and consensus view of reality is the manifestation of the harmony of the unity we all birth from, yet ... it is also an illusion. As eternal consciousness, we designed the human mind to automatically fill in perceived gaps or inconsistencies in our mortal experience. The purpose of the mind—*beyond allowing for unconsciousness to exist*—is to make sense of your experience and assign it meaning.

The mind creates the meaning you live within and forms your unique experience of self.

Any information that the mind is unable to assign an acceptable meaning to is quickly dismissed as not mattering or not being of significance by means of a value judgment.

There are many *dimensions/layers* to reality besides the physical, temporal, mental, and emotional. These layers have become hidden through our choice of beliefs. No external force hid these layers of reality from us. It is we who have come to hide from them (through how we avert our focus away from them).

If we do happen to perceive one of these layers—*in what feels to be a weird, psychic, or magical way*—we have powerful mechanisms that tell us we did not perceive what we thought we just did. These mechanisms primarily operate through the fear of being insane, abnormal, or different (including the fear of being perceived as mad by other people). Additionally, an underlying fear of change can drive our ability to ignore or dismiss what we do not understand. If you evolve your belief system—*by opening your mind*—to include more than is physically apparent, you will start to perceptively translate these '*hidden*' layers into your experience.

> *To meet all that you are, you must be curious,*
> *open to change, and open to new experiences.*

You may emulate a closed system—*a separate individual*—as much as you like; however, beyond your individuated focus, you are an open system. You are a focus of *the one consciousness,* and ALL things flow through you (whether you acknowledge them or not).

To be open is to make fresh choices … and that is to choose change. To be open to change is to be open to the unfolding of *all that you are.* Even when you express *all that you are* into reality, you will still always change because *all that you are,* when expressed into linear time, is an expression of change.

> *You are an evolving journey—not a destination.*

Only a person with a mind that is open to change is open to a reality created in transparency and consciousness. To have an open mind is to be willing to face your fears.

Only a person with an open mind
is open to experiencing the magical
potentials that surround us.

CLARIFICATIONS & REFLECTIONS

Within human form, we have a narrowly focused perception that concentrates on our physical reality, our emotional reality, and our mental reality. This is not to say that we only experience that which is physical, emotional, and mental — it means that no matter what we experience, we translate it into the physical (including temporal, as time-space is one thing), emotional, and mental.

The *'things'* we perceive are not physical or non-physical, emotional or non-emotional, mental or non-mental. Anything that can be perceived can be translated into a physical manifestation, an emotional reaction, *and/or* a mental thought.

To access what may be felt to be the *'hidden'* layers of reality, you do not need any special knowledge or powers. You do not even need to know what to expect. All you need is an open mind — a mind not limited by fear. A mind that is open is curious and seeks what is unknown (instead of fearing it). An open mind assigns space for new meaning (instead of trying to make all experiences fit into what is already known).

A closed mind atrophies through
its need for consistency.

An open mind wants to
expand and change.

With an open mind, it is not that you will suddenly experience a new layer of reality as if someone turned on the light in a dark room. It is that you will start to experience new physical, emotional, and mental sensations that feel slightly *'different.'*

This new level of perception will be subtle at first, such as having memories unexpectedly emerge through which you remember something from a time in your life that offers a meaningful perspective on your current situation. You may also start experiencing a new depth of *emotional excitement* around a particular choice, or an unexpected *emotional resistance* to a particular person (which you cannot see a logical reason for). You may even start to see colors around people or feel the energy in an object (perhaps as a heat-like experience).

It is usually the quality of how it unexpectedly enters your perception that becomes the clearest flag that you are opening your perception.

How you react to that perceived newness/
magic will determine if the experiences
continue to build or are blocked.

CHALLENGE REALITY
WITH WHAT YOU FEEL
IN YOUR HEART

*"I choose to challenge the world
with the love in my heart."*

Do not believe everything reality seems to tell you because your reality reflects not only what you believe but any wounded emotions those beliefs formed around. Reality is not a reflection of *"The Truth"* (a mental notion based on the idea of a solid, objective, absolute, external reality). Your human experience reflects *the self that is present,* including your fears, doubts, and judgments.

*The greatest block within creation is the
belief that something is not possible.*

Through socialization, we each subconsciously absorb many layers of meaning that do not reflect what is in our heart. Therefore, when reality seems to say that what you want is not possible, do not believe it. Take up the challenge to prove reality wrong. This is to feel what is possible from your heart and act from that feeling (instead of allowing yourself to be limited by socialized mental beliefs). To learn to act from your heart—*instead of from what the logic of society tells you*—is to learn to perceive with your most powerful sense.

Do not recognize any limit as absolute.

Even experiences like gravity are continually birthing from our belief in them. *From a purely experiential perspective,* the Earth was flat until someone perceived it as a globe. This is not saying that the Earth was literally flat; it is saying that in terms of meaning, because it was perceived to be flat, the Earth was flat in terms of *our idea of reality.* So, to call it flat was the most accurate description of the reality that was lived within. Those well-trodden pathways in the human psyche remain alive and well in *'Flat Earthers'* today.

To realize the profundity of what is being said here is to discard the limiting idea that there is a solid, objective, external reality and realize that each reality—*in being an illusion*—is only ever *'the idea of itself.'*

This is easier to comprehend with a non-tangible example, such as the belief in *'evil.'* A person who believes in evil lives within a reality with the perceived existence of the presence of evil. Whether or not evil *'really'* exists is irrelevant. If your heart reveals a different message than the one your physical reality seems to be presenting, do not be afraid to challenge your reality and seek to manifest what is in your heart.

To challenge reality is to challenge yourself and break historical patterns/ ruts that no longer serve you.

*Challenge reality with what
you feel in your heart.*

CLARIFICATIONS & REFLECTIONS

Your personal reality is a reflection of *all that you are.* However, in just the same way that you are heavily focused on certain aspects of your spirit in the shaping of your mortal self, your personal reality is also heavily focused on those same aspects. Just as you are a human self couched within the perception of your spirit, your personal reality is also reflectively couched within the wider reflection of your spirit.

Even though we experience ourselves as separate, the wider reality from which we birth is largely within our unconsciousness, with everything perceptively reflected somewhere in our personal reality.

*Every star in the sky could be imagined
as a reflection of a reality that exists
within the one consciousness.*

Our world is couched in this starry sky, just as we are each couched in the collective of humanity. Your personal beliefs —*which reflect the ways in which you have chosen to evolve the collective belief*—exist in relation to the collective, shared belief. For example, if you say, *"I believe I am tall,"* you are saying that you are tall in relation to the collective (because if everyone else suddenly became taller than you, you would no longer experience yourself as tall).

Beyond your personal beliefs, the next most dominant aspect of reality is its reflection of the collective belief system—*which is limited and fear-based*—that your personal beliefs exist in relation to. Even though you are predominantly here to be an individual, you did not come here to create in isolation. Whatever beliefs you are passionate about, you are passionate about them in relation to—*and on behalf of*—the collective of *humanity/the world.*

> *In opening your mind to embrace*
> *what excites you, you will have*
> *to face your perception of the*
> *world's judgment of you.*

When you feel passionate about something that the world seems resistant to, you can always still experience it with those who are ready for it. Choose to focus on people who share your passions. Do not worry about those threatened by them.

UNCONDITIONAL UNIVERSAL LOVE

"I choose to experience myself as both worthy and complete such that I may experience love without need."

Do not fear allowing yourself to love. Being in love has not hurt you. To fear the hurt you will experience if you lose something you love is to fear the effects of attachment and not love. See how easy it can be to blend these feelings. For example, being possessive can feel like a sign of caring.

Learn to distinguish between the feeling of love and the possessive feeling of attachment.

Unconditional love cannot be expressed through attachment. To love someone with conditions is ultimately to disempower them because it is to impose your values and judgments onto that person.

*Attachment is one of the most prevalent
ways we give our power away.*

To become attached to something is to believe you would somehow be less than you are without it. Neither the presence nor the absence of anything can make you more or less than *all that you are.* If a person makes you feel closer to *all that you are,* then it is only because they are expressing an aspect within you that you do not currently perceive as being of you. To love them unconditionally is to open yourself to recognize this aspect in you. If you try to possess them, you will only further cage that aspect outside yourself.

Through attachment, we enter an endless chase to feel complete. This stems from a feeling that we are inadequate, damaged, or missing something.

*To be in a state of attachment is to
have a distorted view of yourself.*

*Whatever it is in life that you want or desire,
the answer is to love it without limitation.*

Every self-created limitation of your love is expressed as a barrier between you and what you love. This reflection is to aid you in removing those barriers so that you may experience *the love that you are* in freedom, rather than limitation.

You can never fully touch anything you are attached to, for you will always be experiencing it through the filter and barrier of your need — your feeling of incompleteness or unworthiness.

To truly touch something is to love it without limitation.

To love without limitation, know with all your heart that you are complete unto yourself.

To love without limitation is to love without need.

To love someone without needing them to be any particular way is to empower them to be *all that you are.*

Universal love is universal empowerment.

CLARIFICATIONS & REFLECTIONS

Because human language has evolved to reflect our polarized perception, it seems logical to think of *unconditional love* as one end of a dualistic polarity (with the opposite end being *conditional love).* While this could reasonably be said to be the meaning of *unconditional love,* to open to the potential of its full meaning is to realize that beyond this dualistic understanding, *unconditional love* is the non-polarized state of connection experienced by your spirit. This understanding encourages us to be open-minded and accepting of *all forms of love,* recognizing that they are all valid and valuable.

To help distinguish unconditional love from its more traditional polarized understanding, it can also be referred to as universal love — a state of equal and unrestricted love for all. Using this term can help depolarize our understanding such that *universal love* is understood to not be superior to, or in opposition to, *conditional love* — it is just different.

Universal love is felt within the conscious awareness of connection.

Conditional love is felt within the experience of unconsciousness—*or partial consciousness*—of connection.

In the same way that our mortal self is not inferior to our spirit, the form that love takes in human form cannot be said to be inferior to the love of our spirit.

Our desire to perceive *universal love* as superior is not because that is how we intrinsically are when we are self-aware — it is a result of our personal judgment of *conditional love*. This is the same as how we can fall into perceiving our spirit as an ideal and our embodied form as something that needs to be fixed or corrected (even though it is our spirit that creates our embodied form).

To enter human form is a choice to experience everything —*including love*—from an individualized perspective. From our spirit's perspective, *'soulmates'* do not exist because it is a possessive form of love. Even if you are not traditionally possessive, calling someone your soulmate instantly labels others as *NOT* your soulmate. And that is a value judgment that separates rather than unifies.

*Universal love connects you with
all, for it is to love all equally.*

MAGICAL SENSES

*"I choose to trust in the guidance I
receive from my inner senses."*

A s space and time are an illusion, your perceptive
senses can operate in ways beyond what is
biologically understood. Much of what you feel as
being impulse, volition, and intuition is you tapping into the
feeling of potentials in your future. This is not about stepping
outside the present moment; it is about bringing potential
experiences into the present moment in a way that helps
direct the flow of your life in accordance with the intention of
your spirit.

*As you step out of the perceptual containment
of linear time, you will experience more of
what you have been and more of what you
will be, all within the present moment.*

To feel what will happen is to look into potential futures by loosening the belief in *linear time* in order to experience the fluidity of *universal time.* The closer you move to being *all that you are,* the more you will experience its state of timelessness and non-definition. This will appear as the opening of your inner senses — the senses that are currently labeled as psychic or magical.

As real as these powers are, they are subject to your belief system — as well as the mass belief system's effect on you. This limitation includes using your inner senses to prove to others that inner senses exist. When you tell someone of your inner experience—*regardless of how emphatic and persuasive you are*—they will always have the free will option to not believe you (maybe by thinking you are deluded or confused). The level of proof available for any phenomenon can only be proportional to the allowance of the mass belief system for it.

> *As the world 'comes to believe,' more proof will become available.*

This *'proof'* is only referring to external consensus proof, not personally experienced proof. Your inner senses can tell you anything with an inner knowing beyond external proof (with that level of knowing being determined by the validity you assign to your inner senses).

> *To learn to trust your inner senses is to learn to trust yourself.*

When you trust in your inner senses, you will find that they grow and expand, leading you on a journey of self-discovery and personal growth. By expanding your experience of reality through inner feeling rather than external proof, you will embark on an incredible journey. This journey, which leads to your *magical/divine/spiritual* self, is a testament to the power of your inner senses and the potential for growth and transformation that lies within you.

> *The allowance of magic is the allowance*
> *of experience that is currently*
> *beyond your understanding.*

> *Know your self as magical, and you will*
> *know magic within your reality.*

CLARIFICATIONS & REFLECTIONS
Our spirit exists outside the restrictive perception that creates the experience of linear time. Instead, it can be thought of as living in a reality of *universal time* — a concept that transcends the limitations of linear time, where all potential experiences are accessible, regardless of any notion of whether they exist in the past or future.

> *Universal time is a state where all*
> *moments, past, present, and future,*
> *exist simultaneously, and our spirit can*
> *access any of these moments at will.*

Because our embodied self seems to be clearly separate from our non-physical spirit, it is easy to assume linear time is just as distinct from universal time as physicality is from non-physicality. The misunderstanding here is that spirit does not experience physicality or linear time (which is to view it as a polarized state).

Your spirit can perceive both physicality and linear time; however, it does not experience itself as contained by them.

Although it does experience them in some fashion, it is very different from the depth of containment that we experience them through while embodied. Our experience of feeling contained within our body is completely different than our spirit's perspective of temporarily experiencing a body that it can transform or discard at will. They are, however, both experiences of physicality (with our perspective seen as deep and our spirits as shallow).

The same shallow-to-deep spectrum
is experienced with linear time
versus universal time.

Linear time and embodiment are most clearly seen as being linked through their experience of containment. Linear time is the perception of the events we experience as occurring in a defined sequence. We experience ourselves as *unalterably connected* to that sequence of events in the same way we feel *unalterably connected* to our physical body.

Within linear time, we feel there is no way to alter what has already happened in the sequence — the past. Often, we feel there is no way to change what is coming up in the sequence —*the future*—whether that be the night, the winter, death, or the need to earn money. We experience ourselves as contained in our temporal sequence in much the same way we feel contained by our embodiment.

Stepping into a shallower experience of linear time is not about foreseeing an unalterable event in a set linear future. It is about opening up to the possibility of multiple potential events and timelines, each of which we can choose to focus on and experience. This shift in perception is not about predicting the future; it is about realizing our potential and the freedom it brings.

SELF-REFLECTION &
SPONTANEITY

*"I choose to allow the experience
of my spontaneous self."*

D o not presume you know everything about who you are, as that is to be in denial that your mortal self is created through selective unconsciousness. To learn to meet yourself is to allow yourself to see yourself from a point of clarity rather than from a point of seeing what you want to see.

*To meet yourself is to view yourself
without preconceptions or agenda.*

Do not be afraid to face yourself in the moment and observe your state of being. To know *all that you are* is not to have arrived at some final destination. It is to realize that you are—*and will always be*—continually meeting yourself through your experience of reality. Learn to meet yourself through your life by being aware in the present without fear for the future or regret for the past.

After every change that unfolds within you, you must meet that change. In meeting how you have changed, you meet yourself anew. Changes are realized through choices.

> *You will know you have changed when*
> *you see yourself making a new choice.*

To know yourself is to recognize exactly *when* you are choosing, *what* you are choosing, and *why* you are choosing it. To become aware of the wider nature of your choices is to become aware of yourself through their reflection.

> *Self-awareness through reflection is a part of*
> *remembering the wider state of consciousness*
> *from which you are continually birthing.*

Although self-reflection has a significant role in our return to consciousness, it is only a tool on the path of awakening — *it is not a superior way of being.* Awakening *includes/affects* the mental, but it is not a mental process. As you step out of the fears through which you have contained your consciousness, you will live in a fluid state of spontaneity rather than a poised state of self-reflection.

> *When fully engulfed in the present moment,*
> *there is no idea of a past or future from which*
> *you can reflect in order to observe yourself.*

When you are not in fear, you are not cautious and naturally allow your experience to be spontaneous. In this state, anything focused on becomes present as there are no temporal boundaries. This is a *'fluid state of spontaneity'*; a state where you are fully present and open to the unfolding of life without the constraints of past or future. To experience more spontaneity in your life is to allow your own freedom.

Embrace the unpredictability of life, for it is in these moments of spontaneity that you most experience your freedom.

Self-reflection is a powerful tool that may aid you in the discovery of your freedom. But, in the moment of that discovery, it becomes obsolete because, without resistance, there is no block to the knowing of *all that you are.*

You must first understand the definition of yourself before you can let go of that definition.

Understanding your self-definition is a stepping stone to understanding the fluidity and freedom of your definition.

CLARIFICATIONS & REFLECTIONS
Trust in and use your sense of direction and the impetus of your volition. Use their input to more easily become whatever definition you feel to become. Embrace the definitions that flow from your joy and see through the distortions of your fear-based perceptions. By exploring and understanding the definitions you purposefully placed in your path, you will awaken to your wider nature and move into the fluidity of non-definition that reflects your spirit.

Freedom consciousness is simultaneously a state of non-definition, an ever-changing definition, and an expression of the equality of all definition.

Freedom is the *no choice* that is inherent in the realization of *all choice.* This is not only to step out of the tightness of individuality you have known, but also to equally appreciate the positive qualities of experience that arise through rigidity and attachment to definition. Only when you appreciate why you chose the hard limits of definition will you cease to resist the rigid definitions through which you have purposefully contained your sense of self.

Embracing fluidity cannot be achieved
through a rejection of rigidity.

See the perfection in your imperfections to step beyond what you have wanted to know yourself to be. Awakening is not about achieving some superior perspective through which you 'ascend from' or 'transcend' your human experience.

To awaken is to see the equality of the
mortal and infinite perspectives such
you are free to move between them.

When speaking to other spiritual explorers, it can be easy to fall into comparing awakening experiences to determine who is 'more awake.' Be conscious of this kind of competitive spiritual hierarchy in your thinking by recognizing how it comes from a fear-based, anxious need within you to 'be more awake.' This need often stems from a fear of *not being good enough* or *not progressing fast enough* on your spiritual journey.

Release the chase for wakefulness by choosing to acknowledge that anyone who realizes the wider nature of their existence beyond the mortal is awake. Beyond this, we are each having our own uniquely personal experience of awakening.

Although they may look very different,
all spiritual paths are of equal value.

LETTING GO OF CONTROL

*"I choose to become conscious
of my need to control."*

The state of allowance includes the realization that you do not need to clutch the steering wheel of life or anxiously watch every bend in the road for hidden obstacles in order to feel safe.

*Enter into a state of allowance by letting go
of the ways you seek to control your reality.*

Do not wait to do this until you are feeling exasperated or as a last resort. Do not do this from a position of testing creation or from anger at *'the Universe.'* Instead, let go of control with complete inner trust and confidence in the existence of the harmony that exists beneath all life — a harmony that will assert itself in the absence of your mental opposition.

*Reality has a powerful fail-safe mechanism to
resolve any situation — the letting go of control.*

Letting go of the effort and pain of needing control can at first sound easy, but, to start with, it may be one of the most exhausting things you have ever done because of how your mind may initially feel adrift and frantic. This reveals how *the need to be in control* stems from a lack of trust in the self and negative beliefs about the nature of reality (such as the belief that life is inherently chaotic or that you are not capable of handling whatever comes your way).

> *When letting go of control brings up fear,*
> *use this as an opportunity to see your*
> *fears more clearly than ever before.*

In doing so, those fears will begin to transform. This will connect you further into your trust of self, as both an incarnate being and a spiritual presence that permeates all life.

To let go of control is to find the place of trust deep inside yourself — the place that is the knowing of *all that you are* (which is the knowing that you are the creator of your reality). This is to feel the flow of life and know that it will take you where you need to go. To let go of control is to know that no external forces can harm you because everything reflects you exploring yourself.

> *The level at which reality emerges*
> *from our consciousness runs far*
> *deeper than our mentality.*

To be the choice-maker in your life does not mean trying to control every aspect of your reality. It can feel good to be '*in control*' — just do not *need* to be in control. To feel the need to control your life is to believe that your life would otherwise be out of control.

Recognize the illusionary nature of control. Do not try to control the results of your choices — make the choices that organically come to you, and then let them go. Let them manifest their own resolution. In this lies the resolution of the paradox of control of your life being simultaneously absolute —*because you are the creator of your life*—and yet an illusion —*because in entering mortality, you choose to be unconscious of your wider nature.*

*Make your choices with confidence,
and then let them go.*

CLARIFICATIONS & REFLECTIONS
Due to our survival mentality, the joy-based, child-like dreams we once had for ourselves become entangled with the experiences we have felt most wounded by. At these times, the energy you exert through the belief that *your fear-based survival mentality is necessary* is the energy that is tightening the knot that makes you fearful. This is usually experienced as the evolution of some kind of obstacle between you and what you think you need to survive.

Learn to recognize these self-created, energetic deadlocks to know when you are being your own impediment. Recognizing yourself as the creator of the block will naturally cause you to stop feeding it with your fear, and the knot you are mentally bound within will begin to loosen.

A beauty of this reality is that if you step back from active creation and allow yourself to fall into the flow of *energy/ consciousness* that underlies—*and fuels*—life, then that motion will always be in the direction of untangling what is tangled, connecting what has become disconnected, and loving what has become unloved.

*Through the release of control, you
enter the state of allowance.*

*This is not an action — it is the release
of action that seeks to control.*

There is nothing you need to learn in order to enter the state of allowance — you must simply to stop acting upon the world (which is to stop trying to control it). However, because we have become so entrenched in acting from a place of control, we often have to remember *how to stop* because we have forgotten what not acting from fear feels like (such that it can feel *unnatural/fear-provoking*).

The connection between allowance and control is made clear through the choice to enter the state of allowance from within a knotted tangle of intentions. In this choice, it can feel as though taking your hands off the steering wheel of life is just as scary as letting go of a car's steering wheel at high speed. Just as your brain tells you not to stop steering your car through the idea that a crash will ensue—*which is helpful for survival in a physical reality*—it will also tell you that your worst fears about what will happen are probable if you do not control every aspect of your reality.

The human mind has become conditioned for survival—*rather than being fruitful*—and that is best achieved by fearfully avoiding negatively perceived outcomes (whereas thriving is best served by joyfully seeking exciting outcomes).

Recognize that control is not wrong. It is simply that when we are unconscious of how we are controlling, we can become a tangle of conflicting intentions (due to the conflicting beliefs across our own internal separations).

THE INDIVIDUAL &
THE COLLECTIVE

"I choose to experience the full spectrum of my being—from my individuated definition to the infinite state of unity consciousness."

Despite how chaotic it may outwardly appear, humanity is collectively moving towards a joy-based Unified Diversity — not a fear-based, conflicting state of diversity. This is to not only know yourself through the singularity of your mortal self but through the *plurality/multiperspective* of the collective.

You are 'the one in the many' and 'the many in the one.'

There is a *'we'—a sense of collective consciousness*—that you can meet within the singularity of the *'I'* of you. You are the blending of a unified expression—*because you are the expression of 'the one which is all'*—with individual conviction. While embodied, you are conquering both the fear of collective consciousness—*feared as being a homogeneous state of 'hive mind'*—and the fear of individuality—*feared as standing alone in what you are.*

> ### Fear of the power of any individual
> ### is fear of your own power.

The conflict created by this paradox is manifested collectively as war. In war, the fear of sharing a unified level of consciousness with everyone is expressed as territoriality, possessiveness, and ownership. This is the fear that your sense of self can be invaded — a reflection of an external fear of invasion.

No individual can have power over you unless you grant it. A person can only appear to have external power when they have convinced others to give over their power to them.

> Love peace … rather than hating, fearing, or trying to control war.

> Honor the right of others to engage in war; do not give them your *power/energy* by trying to prevent it.

> Accept the right of others to have war in order to live in a reality without war.

> ### Warring against war is to feed war.

Accept that you are an individual. Know this as your power, as it means you are the authority in your life because you are the one who makes your own choices.

Accept that you are part of a collective consciousness. Know and feel that you are unified with all within your reality. As we awaken into the state of Unified Diversity, you will experience everyone and *all that they are* directly — just as they will experience *all that you are.*

> *Love and accept yourself to experience*
> *being loved and accepted.*

Do not fear there being no secrets in this state of transparency. In this knowing, love and accept your whole self (because soon there will be no element of it that you can hide).

> *Love yourself in order to be all that*
> *you are, and that is to know and feel*
> *your unity with All That Is.*

CLARIFICATIONS & REFLECTIONS
People often connect the idea of experiencing unity-consciousness with *'high'* drug-related experiences. The experience of *'unity with all existence'* by people taking hallucinogens is not some quirk of human chemistry — it is the clarity of perception experienced when it is not being limited as a means of creating the experience of *individuality/ mortality.*

The main reason these experiences of unity are often written off is due to the *'crazy'* dream-like—*and scary for many*—hallucinogenic experiences that may surround the beauty of unity consciousness. We typically cannot fully accept our resonance with the beauty of feeling unity and discard the more idiosyncratic and quirky experiences as being drug-induced craziness.

What is seen across these altered experiences is that the serene beauty of the unified state of consciousness is the experience most commonly shared, whereas the *'nuttier'* experiences are idiosyncratic and personal.

We all share the joy-based, infinite state of consciousness—the level of our spirit —whereas our personal fears are what individualize and differentiate us.

Taking a drug that causes many of your perceptual filters to be bypassed—*such that you have a direct experience of the wider nature of your consciousness*—triggers some fears that act as a limiting mechanism of the filter (how it blinds). This is why, despite how beautiful the experience of unity consciousness is, it can quickly become overwhelming and is often fearfully interpreted as a threatening invasion of our sense of individuality (which is based on separation from the whole). What is being triggered here is a sense of death itself.

From our mortal perspective, death is feared as an ending when it is, in fact, the point of transformation into your next experience of self.

It is this collision of the open, unified whole with the possessive mortal self within a state of unleashed perception that then creates the *'craziness'* of taking a hallucinogen (because of how the person's fear acts in magnified and highly distorting ways).

If you learn to recognize your fears while in the altered state, you can experience this fluid/ transformative state of consciousness in a more consciously guided, shamanic way.

KNOWING ONLY WHAT
YOU NEED

*"I choose to allow myself to know what
I want to know without needing to
know how I came to know it."*

As mortal beings, we often rely on physical manifestations to understand how we come to know something. However, there are other ways of knowing that do not require such tangible evidence. For instance, you might suddenly *'know'* the answer to a problem without consciously working it out.

*This is a form of knowing that arises from
sources other than observation and deduction.*

For example, you have physically manifested this book into your life, which gives you a physically translated path that describes how you have come to know the ideas you have read within it. Because of this, your logical mind is kept happy in knowing how it came to know these ideas. However, the ideas written in this book were arrived at through an internal experience of simply *'coming to know'* that utilizes the imagination (often called gnosis or channeling).

Despite being more direct, gnosis is not superior in its way of *coming to know* than knowing through outward perception — they are just two different paths to the territory of knowing. Each produces a knowing with slightly different qualities —*all of which contain their own distinct value*—such as the direct—*but intangible*—nature of Gnosticism versus the more circuitous and effortful—*but tangible*—nature of external observation and its logical extrapolation.

> *To be fully aware of your reality is to be*
> *open to BOTH paths to knowing.*

No particular physical experience is required to know the answers to your questions. To begin to allow yourself to know things without the physically manifest path is to allow a more direct and spontaneous experience of creation. This is the *art/ skill/suspension of disbelief* that enables you to allow yourself to know something without *knowing how you came to know.*

> *Can you allow yourself to 'just know' by opening*
> *your imagination to the reality of your spirit?*

This is the realization of what omnipotence in mortal form is. It is not to know the definition of all things simultaneously (which would be disabling within an individualized form). It is to realize that you have the ability to know anything, in any moment, without any restriction, by stepping out of the logic of cause and effect and by allowing yourself to *know without knowing how you came to know.* This is to understand...

Omnipotence is being able to know
whatever you need to know whenever
you need to know it; this is to know
all the knowing you will ever need.

CLARIFICATIONS & REFLECTIONS

The possession of knowledge does not necessarily correlate with awareness. For example, the possession of knowledge predominantly selected from a fear-based perspective leads to a lack of awareness through an imbalance in what you *know/ believe* (usually in the direction of a *pessimistic/cynical/jaded viewpoint).*

Knowing is not about acquiring and
accumulating as much knowledge as possible.

The person with the largest amount of knowledge is not necessarily the most *'knowing.'* Knowing—*in being a quality of self*—does not refer to a state of outward definition; it refers to a state of awareness.

Knowing is a level of awareness characterized by an openness of being to let in and be changed by whatever you focus on through your wish to know it. If you will not accept the change that comes with a knowing, then you cannot know it. To come to know something you did not know is to allow in an experience of change.

The allowance of yourself to change is at
the heart of allowing yourself to know.

However, knowing is not only about embracing awareness (as if it is a superior state). It is also about embracing the existence of not-knowing (because that is a part of allowing who you are in human form). Realize the perspective from which you always know precisely what you need to know to create the desired experience.

This is the understanding that your perspective—*which creates the uniqueness of your experience*—is created from the juxtaposition of what you both *do* and *do not* know about what you are experiencing (because it is created from your ever-shifting state of *consciousness* versus *unconsciousness*).

To reject your level of *'not knowing'* is to choose to experience a denial of your freedom to be (which includes the freedom to not know). It is a denial of the choice to create the individuated form, which is built through an unconsciousness of connection. Similarly, focusing on knowing something you do not need to know can be done to distract yourself from following your inner guidance.

Focus on knowing only what arises through your passion, and you will know everything you *'need'* to know to experience your passion. To focus on knowing something else—*not based on following your heart*—is the choice to experience yourself in limitation.

Allow yourself to not know that which
you do not need to know to fully
experience all the knowing you need.

OUR MASKS & FACETS

*"I choose to embrace and explore
all facets of my being."*

W hat you outwardly portray yourself as believing may not be what you really believe: what you consciously say you want may not be what you really want; how you act may tell a different story than what you say. This highlights the disparity between what you are, what you experience yourself to be, and what you try to project outwardly.

These differing experiences within self are not a fault of the human form; they are a part of how it was designed to operate. Awareness of these levels is not about dissolving them—*as if they were an unwanted problem*—it is about making them conscious choices (rather than levels of *self-denial/self-fear*).

We each play many different roles and have a different face for each role. Do not be afraid to look at the disparity across your many faces. By seeing and naming this disparity, you will better understand the intention behind your focus for this life (through a stronger feeling of what you do and do not resonate with). By identifying your different masks, you will better see what you have chosen to become within embodiment.

> *Only by being willing to see your*
> *masks clearly, can you see the unified*
> *state of being beneath them.*

We are each multi-dimensional beings with many facets. Wearing masks is not wrong. The human form is a mask worn by *the one self/the one consciousness/spirit.*

> *Learn to embrace your faceted nature.*

Recognize the difference between wearing a mask out of fear of who you are without it and wearing a mask to enhance and focus on a particular aspect of your being.

Do not fall into believing that *'to be enlightened'* is to become one consistent, ultimate state of being. Such a belief is a constraint to your exploration of self.

> *Let yourself experience life in many*
> *ways — not in just one way.*

Your faceted nature is a part of the freedom of your being. Feel free to play different characters in the experience of your life. To realize you are faceted is to realize you have the ability to be anything you wish to be, in any way you wish to be it.

A facet is an aspect of a diamond that, although it does possess its own validity, cannot be separated from the whole. Imagine *the one consciousness* as a diamond with an infinite number of facets. No one facet is *the one consciousness,* and yet each facet is an equal projection of the unified whole.

You are an evolving facet of the
one consciousness, a unique part
of a larger, unified whole.

CLARIFICATIONS & REFLECTIONS

One of the most powerful qualities of spirit is its knowing of its connection to all. In this state, there is a sharing of knowing that is—*in relation to what we are in human form*—a state of complete transparency.

Because we tend to think of our spirit as a self that does not wear any masks, we typically conclude that the state of transparency is superior to the state of wearing masks. What this perspective fails to realize is that spirit does wear masks.

Every being in creation wearing a mask is
the one consciousness wearing a mask.

In this context, the *'human form as a mask'* is a metaphor for the idea that our physical bodies and the identities we construct are not the totality of who we are. You are not *'not your spirit'* when in human form — you are your spirit wearing a human mask.

A negative view of masks is heightened through the realization that as we are awakening to how our human form is a mask, a part of awakening does include a clear trend of increasing transparency (as a natural result of moving to reflect our spirit). There is a correlation here to loving peace rather than hating war.

Awakening is about loving transparency;
it is not about rejecting or judging masks
(whether in ourselves or others).

We did not create the human form to *shed it/awaken from it*. To be human is to want to experience at least some level of a mask (otherwise, you would not have left the wider state of consciousness). *Awakening* in this context refers to becoming conscious of the masks you wear and using them in a joyful rather than fear-based way. It is about recognizing the positive qualities of how masks can help us focus and explore particular aspects of our being.

An overt example is an actor's ability to explore human nature by allowing themselves to wear the mask of a character and improvise scenes.

As you awaken to *all that you are*, it can be uncomfortable to become aware of just how many ways you hide your feelings behind fronts or masks. When you allow yourself to openly share feelings you have previously masked, you will naturally find yourself sharing other joyful qualities you did not previously *'let out to play.'*

To drop your mask is not only to face your fears; it is to better meet the joy within you that previously did not feel safe to come out and play (because you had so many masks operating).

TIME AS THE UNFOLDING OF SELF

*"I choose to experience time in a
more open and fluid way."*

E ach moment that you awaken is a further unfolding of *all that you are.* The passage of time is a reflection of your own becoming. It is impossible to go backward, as you are only ever experiencing more and more life … more and more reflections of yourself. The unfolding of the future is your own unfolding. Time is not something *separate/outside of you,* within which you exist.

*You create time to help you describe to
yourself the never-ending unfolding/
awakening of your being.*

The objective measurement of time is only one way of perceiving it. Allow yourself to experience time in other ways. To describe time as a series of seconds and minutes is to describe a beautiful landscape as acreage. To understand that there is a way in which you create your own time is to realize that although there is a fixed quality to external time—*which is determined by physical devices*—there is also an equally powerful *psychological/inner* experience of time.

This psychological subjective experience of time is most acutely felt when comparing the experiences of embracing change—*and life flows easily*—versus resisting change—*and each hour feels like an ordeal.* A person in the flow of life will experience far less psychological time within a given hour—*as determined externally*—than a person struggling. Through the allowance of your openness to change, you are the one who determines the rate at which you experience time inwardly.

> *Time is that which allows the*
> *experience of becoming.*

To realize that time is but a tool—*used by consciousness in the creation of its experience*—is to take power over the rate of your own unfolding. Every person runs at their own speed. What one person may experience in a day may take another person a month. To experience something at different speeds is to experience it with a different result.

> *Faster is not better than slower;*
> *it is just different.*

Whether a person lives for days or years, at the end of their life, they will have lived for a lifetime and experienced all they wanted to experience in that form. Time is a quality of manifestation — not a framework into which manifestation must fit.

*Every mortal self lives the same
amount of time — one lifetime.*

CLARIFICATIONS & REFLECTIONS

The scientific view of time accurately describes the way in which we experience linear time as external, objective, and independent of us.

> *For example, if two people meet at a set time and location, start their stopwatches, and agree to meet 24 hours later, their stopwatches will still be synchronized when they meet again, even if they have vastly different psychological experiences.*

Stopwatches only measure the amount of physical time that has passed. They do not measure how much psychological time—*the feeling of time*—has been experienced.

> *For example, a person who became lost in a creative project for the day would have felt the time fly by, whereas a person who struggled with a crisis would have felt as though a couple of days had passed because they were so exhausted.*

We see physical time as '*real*' and psychological time as a vague concept with little value; this is an understandable response because of how we have chosen to organize our existence around outward physical time (because it is extremely helpful for synchronizing outward events).

That said, our collective focus on the objective experience of physical time does not need to preclude us from exploring our subjective experience of time. This exploration could involve mindfulness practices, meditation, or simply paying more attention to our internal experience of time.

*For example, with death through the body wearing out,
psychological time is a better predictor of lifespan than
physical time. A person who lives within reality as a
beautiful dream with days flying by will live longer than
a similar physical body, experiencing a drama-filled life
where each day feels like climbing a mountain. If these
two people were to meet each day, their stopwatches
would perfectly match. Yet, if aging was measured by
how worn out the body was, one will have aged faster
than the other.*

Physical time is as science describes; it is what time is when
you measure it with physical devices. However, as you awaken
to the wider perception of your eternal consciousness,
you will recognize that internal subjective experiences of
consciousness and objective experiences perceived as external
are of equal value.

To become a master of time has nothing to do with
manipulating stopwatches.

*Being a master of time is about
understanding consciousness as the
creator of our experience of time.*

DREAM AS A CHILD

*"I choose to dream, fantasize, and
imagine with the freedom of a child."*

As we grow up, we accumulate an array of both positive and negative experiences. This accumulation of emotional charges makes our beliefs about the world both positive and negative. This causes us to *be polarized/view reality in a polarized way.*

As adults, we evolve our belief system to help us navigate the world by identifying and avoiding painful experiences and steering toward joyful experiences. As such, our personal sense of self feels identified with our belief system and sees it as a representation of who we are. However, despite how helpful and hard-earned our accumulation of knowledge— *and its associated beliefs*—can feel to be in terms of effectively navigating society, we typically do not notice how this causes us to disconnect from the infinite freedom of our imagination.

To perfect a skill—such as navigating reality through the choices we make—is to become like a perfect hammer. There is nothing wrong with this. However, there is much more to the human experience than banging in nails effectively. Life is not a test; it is an invitation.

Life is an invitation to play.

Feel how your childhood dreams still exist within you, even when you have lost contact with the knowing of *your freedom to be* which you had as a child. To devalue your imagination is to close your heart. When we do this as a part of *'becoming an adult,'* we are then the only ones who can choose to open ourselves back up to the play of dreaming again with the freedom of unrestricted fantasy.

To remember this aspect of you is not just a choice to allow ourselves to roam freely through our imaginations once more; it is the choice to take an empowered position over our most painful experiences. To reawaken *the child* within you, you must let it meet *the adult* in you.

To choose to live in joy is to choose to release the past — including the feelings of guilt, shame, sacrifice, and a sense of mission within it.

Are you willing to unknow your pain as you have known it by no longer identifying it as a wound? There is no knowledge you need to accumulate to keep yourself protected. There is no fear you cannot perceptively transform and release. To live in joy is to walk freely within reality, such that you see past its masks and live through your feeling for life.

The most exciting experiences of self are present in joy and call you from within the many probable realities before you. Between you and that joy stands whatever fear you are carrying (embedded in your body and beliefs). To walk through that fear is to uncloak it, which is to uncloak yourself from the negative fear-based beliefs you may have developed as a form of self-protection.

> *To be fearless is not 'to not know fear'; it is to*
> *not be contained by the negative experiences*
> *of your past that led you to become fearful.*

CLARIFICATIONS & REFLECTIONS

Although it may seem there is a positive message to *'dream big'* in this world, as we grow up, this message is doused in warnings not to be naïve and to keep our dreams realistic, practical, and based on financial productivity. Through this counter-message to *'dreaming big,'* we are taught to bury the magnificent fantasies we fostered in our childhood in order to get down to the business of working hard to earn money and fulfill our obligations.

Just because the dreams you carried in your heart as a child are a part of a child's innocent wonder does not mean they do not have value or need to be grown out of.

> *Our childhood wonder-filled dreams do*
> *not naturally die as a part of growing up*
> *— we actively choose to suppress them.*

These fantasies—*birthed free from restrictive beliefs*—exist like a child within us ... a child who has not been conditioned to think in small and limited ways. This child represents the creative power of choice — a level of self free from the *'adult'* filters of practicality, logic, duty, the past, or knowing the right thing to do.

Remember your childhood fantasies to experience once again what it is to dream as a child. To resurrect this gift is to allow the child within you to exist again through the allowance of your imagination to roam freely and your body to act and play in that fantastical landscape without regret, guilt, or shame.

Remember what it is to be someone who does not think in terms of right and wrong, should and shouldn't, or within ideas of what is and isn't possible. Without the restrictive idea of *needing to know* in order to act, you will naturally dance and play freely in the present moment.

> *Joy arises in the presence of clarity ... in this state, there are no mistakes because the value of everything is seen and appreciated.*

As you recognize how painful experiences in your youth, such as bullying, rejection, or loss, caused you to develop fearful ideas about the world, see how the fears that have most haunted you are a repetitive mental state of perception. When you disarm your fears by seeing them in this way, know you are capable of meeting any fear as an exciting sensation to explore and learn from rather than as an obstacle to be defeated.

INDIVIDUALITY VERSUS UNITY CONSCIOUSNESS

"I choose to embrace the full diversity within myself—that which spans the full spectrum of experiences from unity consciousness to individuality."

Within us, there is a dynamic interplay between our individuality, which is shaped by our physical form, and the unity consciousness we experience beyond the physical realm. The non-physical state of unity is often depicted as a divine, harmonious utopia. This portrayal implies that we should naturally desire to transcend our human form and embrace our spiritual essence. This perspective presents a paradox.

To view *unity consciousness* as superior to *individuality,* one must be within the polarized state of *individuality* rather than the inclusive perception of *unity consciousness.* This paradox challenges our traditional beliefs and invites us to reconsider our perspective.

What we as individuals perceive as the quality of unity is not experienced without the *relative position/vantage point* of our individuality. Without the separation of individuality, there is no quality of *not being unified* against which we can experience the quality of *being unified.*

You have the capacity to experience both
unity consciousness and individuality;
this recognition is a key part of awakening
to the wider nature of consciousness.

This realization marks the end of feeling confined by the experience of individuality. Instead, the experiences of unity consciousness and individuality become like an internal perceptual staircase. You can ascend or descend this staircase depending on whether you seek a unified or individuated perspective on what you are perceiving. This fluidity in the experience of self serves as a bridge between the contrasting experiences of separation and unity that are always present within the human experience.

Opening this level of percpetion
liberates you from the constraints
of a fixed perspective.

To release any fears or doubts you have that becoming embodied was not your choice, recognize that unity consciousness and individuality are of equal value. Open yourself to the perspective that they are not separate but two ends of a single pool of consciousness — with both ends expanding through their relative experience of each other.

Feel the unity that exists across our human individuality and know it as a part of you. To become human is not only to become physical; it is a state of consciousness bridging the non-physical and the physical.

We are each unified consciousness transforming itself through the creation of our diverse experience of being human. This unity is a powerful reminder that we are all part of a larger whole, connected in ways that transcend our individual experiences. It is this interconnectedness that makes our human experiences so rich and meaningful.

CLARIFICATIONS & REFLECTIONS
Through personal experiences of unity from within embodiment—*the feeling of being at one with everything*— the feeling of unity can often seem more desirable than the feelings of separation and isolation that can be felt within physical form. However, understand that the consciousness you are is already present within the unity—*because the unified state of consciousness encompasses all time and space*—even if you, as an individual, are currently choosing to perceive yourself as disconnected from it.

The feeling of separation that we often experience as humans is a part of the illusion of this world. In reality, there is nothing from which we are truly separate. Recognizing our experience of separation as purely perceptual means understanding that there is nothing to *'return to'* because we never truly left.

You cannot return to where you already are.

What you seek is neither a return to a previous state nor an ascension to a higher plane of existence. Awakening is the conscious realization that you are already where you seek to be. You already have what you want — to experience being human.

The state of *'being awake'*—*which ideas of ascension or enlightenment seek to point you to*—is best described as a *remembering* of *all that we are* (rather than the discovery of *all that we are*). This concept of *'awakening'* as a process of *remembering,* not discovering, is to recognize that it is fully available to you right now. However, this does not mean there is not an experience of discovery within the wider experience of remembering — for to remember from within a state of forgetting is an experience of relativity that those who never forgot their connection to everything do not have.

> *'To awaken' to unity consciousness from within the forgetting of individuality is to experience something new in remembering something old.*

> *We are each a new perspective on something anceint and eternal.*

What is being pointed to is how individuality and unity consciousness are created through an interplay of *consciousness* and *unconsciousness* — which is experienced as *known* and *not-known.* What we are when embodied is not a state of pure individuality — it is one state of consciousness that includes both the experiences of individuality and unity consciousness. And, if you become aware of the illusory nature of separation, you will experience yourself as existing in relation to them *both.*

THE MAGIC OF YOUR UNIQUENESS

*"I choose to experience and express
what makes me unique."*

Perceiving the power and profundity of your uniqueness is part of understanding the paradoxical quality of being a separate individual while simultaneously being a free and equal expression of *the one consciousness.*

No other person is exactly *as you are* or experiences exactly *as you do.* Although we are all fundamentally equal, you are the best—*which is to say 'unequaled'*—at being you. No one can ever be more you than you. Your unique expression is a testament to your individuality and a powerful tool that can inspire and empower others.

*You are the best at being you, and that
is what makes you truly unequaled.*

Do not be afraid of what makes you unique, both in terms of your outward definition and your inner experience of consciousness. To allow yourself to travel into your uniqueness is to travel deeper into *all that you are.* This is the awakening of your magical self because of how it incorporates your full inner senses (which we are taught to shut down in childhood).

The outer reality we share is only one aspect of our personal reality — it is only one facet of *all that we are.* To allow yourself to experience all sides of your being is to allow the unfolding of what makes you unique into your experience of reality. It is to allow—*predominantly through your inner senses*—qualities of experience that are subtle, magical, and not easily articulated.

To further unfold the potential of *all that you are* is to have reached a point of self-awareness through which you are comfortable in who and what you are. From this arises an assuredness of self such that you can turn away from the safety of the familiar, shared, consensus view of reality and experience the unconstrained magical self.

Your magical self is the part of you that is unique, creative, spontaneous, and fearlessly unbound by societal norms. To allow your magical self is to allow back aspects of your beingness that you suppressed as a child — usually because of how they made you feel too different or separate.

Do not fear being alone in your uniqueness.

Your uniqueness is not a barrier, but a bridge that connects you to others who appreciate and value your individuality. You are not alone in your uniqueness, but a part of a diverse *community/collective* of other unique individuals. To release the fear of *being alone in what you are* is to have the courage to express the qualities of consciousness that others do not allow themselves to experience.

It takes courage to step out of the norm and share what is new and different.

Courage is a testament to your determination to be true to yourself, regardless of societal expectations. See the value in sharing what is new and different rather than what is traditional and the same.

Sharing your uniqueness with the world will separate you from it just as much as it will unify you with it (because of how you will experience yourself reflected in the polarization of its perception). Do not fear this. Do not fear standing in front of the world. To embrace and share your uniqueness is to deepen your relationship with the world by more clearly being *who you already are* (regardless of the world's reaction).

CLARIFICATIONS & REFLECTIONS
Your magical self cannot be met through the analysis of the mind. Our minds have largely been built on the consensus view of what this world is. However, your magical self is not limited to your knowing of *this* world — it is of *all* worlds. To experience it is to step deeper into what makes you unique.

What makes you unique may not have any language associated with it.

Our language is not as free and precise in its ability to describe experience as we often believe (a phenomenon translators frequently experience) because of how it has evolved to describe what is common and shared (rather than what makes us different and unique).

To find the language to express yourself is to create the words through which you can express the full spectrum of the diverse qualities within you. To create those words in language is to create inner worlds within the shared experience. By finding the right words, you can articulate and share your unique experiences and perspectives, enriching both your own understanding and that of others.

Create words to create worlds.

This is a reflection of the gift that you will choose to share with the world when you overcome the fears you have of loving, embracing, and being yourself.

As much as this book may lead you to focus on understanding how we are all one consciousness, it is equally important to focus on how we are all choosing to experience ourselves as different.

To view the limitations that make you unique as purposeful choices leads you to experience the ways in which you may feel you are lacking in a whole new light. Rather than seeing yourself as a mixed bag of qualities—*some of which you are naturally proficient at and others which you find difficult*—view all your qualities as the result of meaningful choices made to guide and shape your finite, mortal experience in this infinite playground.

Experience yourself as being who you intended to be rather than someone flawed who has no choice but to *'make the best of it'*. Do not do this from a place of loving yourself *despite* your limitations — love yourself for being the embodiment of the state of consciousness who wisely knew to choose your idiosyncrasies.

TRANSFORMING
THE PAST

*"I choose to transform any negative perception
of my past by creating an empowered
experience of it in my present."*

As you walk further into freedom, you will naturally release any emotional baggage you are still carrying. A state of wounded consciousness is not compatible with the state of freedom consciousness — the knowing of yourself as the creator of your reality. As a result, the unfolding of freedom is, to begin with, predominantly a process of releasing stuck negative emotions—*connected to the past*—and their associated beliefs (beliefs that no longer have a role to play in your free-flowing present).

Awakening is initially experienced as a transformation of your perception of your present self through the transformation of your perception of your past experience. This is a feeling of your past experience collapsing into an empowered present understanding.

Without an awareness of this process—*which unearths all your emotional wounds for release*—it is easy to believe that you are doing something wrong or have made a mistake when yet another painful feeling emerges. This can lead to the wounded feelings being repeatedly repressed—*instead of transformed*—with the wound continuing to *affect/limit/focus* your present experience in ways you are not conscious of.

To release a difficult wound from the past—*even though it can be painful to re-experience*—is pleasing when we meet it through the understanding that an emotional weight you have been carrying is finally being laid to rest (the joy of releasing a heavy burden). This level of self-awareness can only happen when you stop judging what you are experiencing and instead treat it purely as an experience to learn from in a positive way.

No feeling within you requires your judgment.

Allow yourself to feel your experience without applying a mental charge, and you will hear and integrate its message. This will lead you to understand why you created whatever you were resisting.

When the past comes up within you,
meet it through the clarity of your
present state of awareness.

There is nothing you need to do except allow yourself to *feel whatever you feel, whenever you feel it.* Allow your feelings to hear their message. Allow your experience to see the wisdom of its creation. The less you resist your pain—*by not falling into judgment, shame, guilt, or regret*—the easier its release will be.

The past is like a piece of subjective art that you carry around, and only you can choose to elevate and empower your perception of it.

CLARIFICATIONS & REFLECTIONS

To awaken from within our embodied form is to become more conscious of who and what you are. In full consciousness, we see that pain is only experienced in states of unconsciousness (which allows for the denial that we are the creator of our experience). All that we describe as negative, painful, or wounded within us can only arise from the unconsciousness of what we are.

Awakening is to make clear and conscious what is being experienced through the distortion of our chosen form of unconsciousness. This is often referred to in spiritual literature as...

...the path of making the unconscious conscious.

To awaken is to transform a past state of perception characterized by unconsciousness into a present state of perception characterized by consciousness. The transformation of a past wound can only take place in the present, and that means re-meeting it where you left it.

You will find your unresolved energies at the point when your perception became so painful that you looked away and became a victim of the event (as opposed to standing in the knowing of it as a self-created experience). This is to allow yourself to re-experience the pain, which will then mark the moment when you can make a different choice and perceive the event as an empowered creator rather than a wounded victim.

The most common stumbling block to this process is the belief that if you are successfully healing yourself, you should be continually feeling better and better. Insisting on this kind of constant linear progression does not allow for bringing our past wounds back into the present so that they can be transformed.

This can particularly be an issue for those who interpret *the law of attraction* to mean that all negative-feeling experiences should be avoided or rejected. To transform a wounded perspective within such a deep experience of linear time, we must walk back through the experiences that the wound formed around.

> *Do not fear inviting your past back in*
> *— it is a part of your beauty.*

THE POTENTIAL
OF HUMAN LIFE

*"I choose to open myself to both perceive
and receive whatever most excites me in the
infinite potentials that surround me."*

To say that you are the creator of your own experience
is to say that only you can choose to create the dream
that exists within your heart. You are not obligated
to create this imagining of reality, and there is no penalty for
ignoring its existence within you. However, understand that
this fantastical dream birthed from your spirit and is the basis
from which your human life emerged — as such, it represents
your clearest available path to joy within this world.

Creating your dream is not like having an empty plot of land
on which you build a house by purchasing and assembling its
components. Your dream for this life is one of desired feelings.
It is not a dream of the definitions you think will evoke those
feelings.

You did not birth here to create definition in a vacuum —
you sought to create something not only *within* the human
experience but *from* and *of* the human experience. All that
humanity is and can be is the clay for your creation.

*Humanity is not an obstacle to be overcome in
order to create something separate from it.*

You are here to create a human — you.

Just as the seed of a flower is encoded energy ready to blossom
its beauty, so every unfolding event in your life is a seed of
potential that you can choose to weave into your personal
dream of what this reality can be.

These potentials that surround you are the energy to
create your dream.

They are the bearers of your choices — the vessels
through which your choices will unfold.

They are freedom cloaked in definition, waiting to
blossom their message of liberation.

They are the movement through meaning—*via
choice*—through which you can transform your
reality.

Every potential we ever meet is made personal through how
it reflects the energy of our choice to birth into human form.
Each of the potentials that surround you carries its own
unique flavor. Whatever you focus on will unfold, and you will
begin to integrate it. Choose what excites you, and the seed of
that choice will start revealing its gift.

*To allow that blossoming is to
further birth your dream.*

To resist a blossoming is to simply re-wrap the choice so that it reappears in a different guise for you to choose another day.

Your choices are not a test unless you choose to make them so. The human experience is one that you can play within and discover yourself. Although being human be a challenging experience, you are not within a test.

You are within a playground of self-discovery.

CLARIFICATIONS & REFLECTIONS

Creation unfolds through our choices. These are met through the experience of realizing what we can potentially be. To choose to focus on a potential is to unfold its gifts into your life by receiving experience through your chosen focus.

To fully receive anything, you must be open to it. Experience yourself as a receiver of creation because that is what you are. You are a creative receiver. You are creating by making the choice of which of the surrounding infinite potentials you want to unfold and receive.

You are feeding yourself your focus.

You are integrating your focus.

Being open is a state of allowance. However, a desire to allow is not enough. You can only *receive/perceive* that which you are able to believe is possible. Though experiences shape your beliefs, those experiences do not choose your beliefs.

You are the determinant of what you believe.

Rigid beliefs create a small aperture of reception through which experiences tend to feel limited and predetermined. Free your beliefs to widen this aperture such that you are able to experience miraculous potentials. You are not just a receiver but a creative receiver, shaping your reality through your beliefs and perceptions.

All perception is a creative choice.

Your senses are not only perceivers of experience. They are creators of experience because of the way in which they—*based on what you have chosen to believe*—automatically reduce that which is infinite in potential into that which is perceived as absolute and definite.

Allow your beliefs about yourself and this reality to expand and blossom such that life experiences coming through your portal of perception reflect your dreams of what can be rather than your fears of what is. By perceiving everything as being within a state of unfolding potential—*as opposed to a fixed thing that you must choose to change*—see how we are each, in every moment, making profound life choices through the choice of what we are focusing on.

Open yourself to receive the limitless potential of your creative self.

Embrace the belief that miracles are not just a possibility but a reality waiting to be birthed by your choices and actions. You have the power to manifest the miracles you have dreamed of, and they are closer than you think.

Give birth to the love that you are.

You are a miracle giving birth to yourself.

THE JOY OF WANTING

"I choose to joyfully create what I want and feel the joy of wanting all that I choose to create."

Many people believe that *desire/wanting* is the cause of suffering and, therefore, understandably, want to demonize it. Wanting something, in and of itself, does not cause pain, but it is a vessel through which your emotional wounds can be experienced. This is akin to saying that pain is not an inherent part of love, but through a focus on unrequited love, we can experience our feeling of love as being a vessel for an intensely painful experience. The choice to stop loving because of this possibility is valid as there are no *'wrong'* choices, but to view it consciously is to understand that it is a fear-based choice to limit your experience.

There is nothing 'wrong' with wanting.

Wanting is a part of the creative process through which not only all realities come into being but through which you also come to be living this life (through the wanting of your spirit to experience). However, it is important to be aware when this *wanting* has become a *need* because it is coming from a place of fear or wounding.

You can do this by becoming aware of the space within you that you would call *'where I want to be'* or *'I will be happy when.'* Feel into the ways in which you need something to be different from the way things currently are. Next, allow yourself to feel any pain you are carrying in relation to these feelings, and you will become aware of the ways in which you are resistant to yourself.

Whether you experience your wanting as positive or negative is a choice that can be felt as either an exciting anticipation of what could be or as a depressing focus that constantly reflects what you believe you lack.

Pain only arises when your desires mentally separate you from experiencing the beauty and perfection of your current reality because of how *'what is wanted'* becomes a symbol of what you do not have and of what you do not believe you have the power to choose (instead of motivating you towards a potential creation).

Love-based wanting is not just a state; it is a transformative force. It is an attractive state based on the desire to love — not a state of fear or rejection. When you operate from this state, your desires are not mere wishes but powerful intentions that can shape your reality. It is a state that inspires, not intimidates. It is about desiring from a place of abundance, not lack. It is a state that empowers you to create the reality you desire.

> *Love-based wanting is about wanting because*
> *you love, not wanting because you fear.*

Embracing your desire is not a sign of weakness but a powerful acknowledgment of your inner truth. It is a choice to love your reality and meet your feelings of want free from the distorting effects of fear.

Your choice for this life was not a mistake. Feel the pain connected to any belief that this life is not where you desire to be. Release any grief you are carrying about the state of your reality—*by recognizing it as a state of attachment*—and see it anew as an invitation to create (instead of as a statement of what you lack).

> *Embrace your desire—do not fear it—*
> *because it tells you why you chose this life.*

CLARIFICATIONS & REFLECTIONS

To see your feelings of want clearly is to see what you joyfully desire, instead of what you fearfully believe you need in order to survive or be happy. Explore the idea that *there is nothing you need to do or receive* in order to fulfill your intention for this life.

Discover what new ideas birth from this expansive space, and observe what thoughts act to hold you from it. Contemplate any idea that seems to tell you what you need to do or what you must act on to resolve it.

> What is it in yourself, in others, in the world that you must fix?

> What do you believe needs to be done, and how does that exist in relation to what you want to do?

To allow yourself to see the difference between *what you want* and *what you believe* you need is to allow yourself to see what holds you back from being in the state of freedom consciousness that your spirit exists in. It is to face your self-defining judgments, and that is to shine a light on the unsettled aspects of your beingness that arise when you let go of fighting your reality. Outward drama is an external surface-level distraction from what is unsettled internally.

To be awake is to be free.

An aspect of being free is knowing there is nothing you need to do; there is only what you joyfully want to do. This carries no sense of attachment to any *'when,' 'where,'* or even *'if'* it happens. In wakefulness—*without mental fears overlaying your perception*—there is no *'I need'* or *'I must have.'* Feel your consciousness free of both fear and need, and you will see how they are but two disguised faces of emotional wounds.

Feeling without attachment to outcome is free-flowing and profound. Feeling without attachment shatters the definitions through which we tend to guide our choices. Our self-definition can easily become what we believe we must do with our life — usually through the idea that doing it will make us more valuable, deserving, or worthy. You do not need to do anything to be of value, and any value you experience based on what you have done can only ever be a transitory experience of fulfillment.

Freedom consciousness is not about doing whatever you want but about realizing that there is no force, no beingness, and no morality that requires you to do anything. There is no requirement to be. When you let go of attachment to outcome, you experience a profound sense of peace and liberation. Consciousness is free.

There is nothing you need to do to awaken, to be happy, or to be free.

EMBRACE WHAT YOU FEAR

*"I choose to explore all aspects
of whatever I fear."*

Allow yourself to experience and explore whatever you fear about yourself, including your fear for your future; do this so you can work on the fear directly in reality, instead of with your mental idea of it.

As long as you avoid meeting what you fear—*which is rejecting an aspect of yourself*—then that fear will operate within you, leading you to unconsciously overlay your perception with a negatively charged, polarized perspective. This is to be wounded by an emotionally painful event in your past, such that you cannot stop it from affecting your perception of your present.

*Free yourself from your wounding
by turning and facing whatever you
have been running from.*

Turn and face your fears knowing they cannot harm you — because they are a part of you (just in disguised form). To meet your fears takes courage, but when that state of transformation is engaged, it is discovered to be an experience of walking into your freedom (rather than into the bottomless well of pain it is feared to be).

To meet and transform an inner fear is not simply to clear a wound; it is to meet an experience of change inside yourself.

This change is not a reversion to who you were before you were wounded. It is a reflection of whatever positive aspect you had to focus inside of yourself to transform the wound.

When the reality of this change is understood, you will become aware that the fear you transformed to heal yourself was always present, masking a fear of the change you have gone through. At the heart of all fear—*even our primal fear of death*—is the fear of how something will change us.

To embrace change is to allow the release of our unconscious mental constraints. It is a step towards liberation ... a step towards a more authentic and free self.

To summon the courage to meet your fears is to realize that you both *are* and *are not* what you fear — because *you are all things.* You are weak and ineffectual, and you are strong and effective. You are selfish and greedy, and you are selfless and generous.

You are all things, and that is to say that you are no thing in particular.

The potential of all qualities exists within you. This is what freedom is. All that can be experienced and expressed is available for you to choose — it is available for you to be. The limitless potential that is experienced by embracing the relativity of great awareness, as well as profound unconsciousness, is yours.

> *Do not fear this breadth of being —it*
> *simply means we use both love and fear*
> *to create our mortal experience.*

CLARIFICATIONS & REFLECTIONS

Overcoming your fears is about realizing that what you have come to fear inside of yourself—*your fear-based thoughts*—is not fully founded in reality. If you face the reality you fear, you will understand the ways in which your fear-based beliefs were creating an imbalanced perspective. This process of seeing through *the lie within your fears* is what most people initially experience when they face their fears. However, facing your fears is not only about realizing the ways in which they are not true.

To step out of polarized perception is to become aware that all things—*regardless of what we call their intrinsic qualities*—can be viewed from both positive and negative perspectives. Fear is where we have become so consumed by the negative perspective that we no longer focus on the positive perspective.

Facing a fear is not about the positive perspective negating the negative perspective (which would be the belief that you were *'wrong'* to view it from the negative, but now are *'right'* to be viewing it from the positive). It is about seeing that *both* perspectives contain equal potential for awareness and blindness because *both* perspectives are limited compared to the full-spectrum joint perspective (that includes both the positive and negative *vantage points/reflections*).

This full-spectrum perspective—*which is analogous to the infinite perspective or your spirit*—is not about realizing that your fears about yourself are completely untrue. It is about realizing that these fears represent a partial state of truth. What you fear is within you is potentially within you, but *it is not what you are* unless you choose to exclusively focus on it (and, even then, it is only what you are for the duration of that focus).

All that you fear is a part of your potential, and it is not wrong or a mistake to consciously explore that potential (or to have chosen to be unconsciously possessed by that fear).

> *If you aspire to be wholly free, your freedom must encompass all things.*

This is the essence of *freedom consciousness,* the core of our being, irrespective of the form we inhabit.

> *Your freedom must transcend your fears and loves and extend to the boundless realm of choice.*

TRANSFORM YOUR OPPONENTS

*"I choose to become aware of the obstacles
and opponents as choices for experience
rather than as unwanted trials."*

We have developed powerful mental mechanisms to process and deal with the many illusions of this reality — such as the illusion that an adversarial force can stand against us. These mechanisms become identifiable patterns of consciousness and are recognized as aspects of our mortal self.

Some of these aspects have become deeply ingrained, such as the part of us that feels it has to either work hard or fight against an opponent to get what it wants. However, if you are now stepping into freedom consciousness, these aspects must either transform with your reality or be released.

This transformation occurs by seeing the positive shadow created by having an opponent — such as the evolution of the courageous hero fighting injustice, the wise teacher fighting ignorance, or the loving healer battling disease. These roles have served us well; however, as we release *'the opponent,'* these aspects will start to feel their redundancy. This often creates an unconscious desire within us to give these courageous aspects something to do such that the positive feelings they generate can reinforce our feeling of self-worth.

> *Having an opponent to contend with*
> *is not solely a negative experience;*
> *it serves as a tool for self-definition*
> *and a means of self-validation.*

Overcoming a challenge is a way to feel safe by demonstrating your ability to fend off an attack. It is a way to focus, witness, and recognize your strength when you doubt it. The empowerment felt through rising to a challenge becomes a testament to your resilience and capability, making you feel strong and capable.

> *The world without an*
> *opponent is not all rosy.*

Initially, your life may feel quiet and empty because your path is no longer dictated by your fear-based reaction to external forces. Even with the world of wonderment, opportunity, and freedom that opens up, it is important to recognize that you will, on some level, miss the feeling of fighting to overcome a limitation.

Become aware of the aspect of you that craves a spicy drama, a battle to be won, or a foe to vanquish. This is to recognize how what you once hated has, in fact, always been serving you.

> *We have always been free because*

*we have always been the ones who
have chosen our opponents.*

Our creation of the opponent is the reflection of our creation of the polarized perception on which the human experience is founded. To even conceive of an opponent is a mirable to *the one consciousness.*

*To see this is to love your opponent as
you love yourself; it is to see how you
have created this world together.*

CLARIFICATIONS & REFLECTIONS
The obstacles of this lifetime are not an unfortunate or unavoidable side effect of birthing into this kind of space-time individualized reality. In choosing to enter the human experience, you are not trying to rectify some out-of-control experiment.

> You are not here to save the world from its shadows or limitations (though you are free to have that experience within yourself).

> You are not here to resolve the world's negatively charged perceptions (though you are free to do that within yourself).

> You are not here out of any sense of commitment, duty, or mission (though you are free to have these mental ideas drive you).

> You are here because it excites you to experience all that being human is (which includes the many diverse ways in which having a challenging opponent or obstacle to overcome is invigorating).

We are the consciousness that created this experience (both as a whole and at a personal level). Every obstacle you have overcome is of your own design, and you chose its exact form with great wisdom. Every opponent you have faced was chosen with great love and care.

To recognize this love and wisdom is to see the way in which it expands your understanding of not only yourself but also what consciousness is within an individualized state of polarized perception (the mortal experience). This is to experience the joy of your inevitable expansion, which is to know that each and every event in your life—*no matter how difficult*—was a moment you wanted to experience.

To see an obstacle or opponent as a chosen journey of expansion is to step from the state of victimhood into the state of conscious creatorship (victims are still creators; they are just unconscious of it). When you see your difficulties free from the energy of victimhood, much of what was previously experienced as negative is transformed, and the joy of seeing how you will handle the situation is revealed.

> *Hear the message within the choice to experience your greatest obstacles in order to transform them (and be changed by them).*

Every trial in your life is a journey that you lovingly planned for yourself. See the gifts of your chosen journey, and you will see the choice to stand within the empowerment of your creatorship. To know why you have created *'all that has made it difficult for you to believe you are the creator of your reality'* is to know your spirit, mortal self, and intention for this life.

RELEASING SACRIFICE

"I choose to release sacrifice
and debt from my life."

I n a hierarchical world with limited resources, to make a
sacrifice for another person is perceived as being both
noble and loving. This comes with the belief that the
greater the sacrifice, the greater the demonstration of love.
Though an act of sacrifice may indeed be associated with
a deep feeling of love when it is understood that 'we are all
one'—with our intentions for this life coming from a common
place—it is seen that no dream for this life is made to be
sacrificed to allow for another.

*All intentions align because
they all birth from the will of
the one consciousness.*

Even though making a sacrifice for someone may outwardly
aid them (and they may even tell you how they needed you to

do this for them), all ideas around the need to make sacrifices arise from limited fear-based beliefs. Although this does not mean that making sacrifices for others is a mistake, it does mean that the love within your sacrifice is always counter-balanced through the reinforcement of the shadow belief in self-limitation.

To sacrifice something for another person is to sacrifice a part of your freedom to be yourself because of the way in which it entrenches our belief in the need for—*and nobility of*—sacrificing our dreams. This has been a meaningful part of our experience but one that cannot persist as we collectively move into freedom consciousness.

> *Unconditional love emerges from*
> *freedom consciousness; it does not*
> *compromise, harm, or limit.*

If your action in any way makes a sacrifice of your being, then regardless of how loving you may feel, there is a fear-based belief being expressed through that love. Even though your sacrificial action may outwardly appear to aid someone, it has not only freed them, it has also limited them in how it has taught them that the solution to their dilemma was not something already within them but could only be found within the sacrifice of another person (reinforcing the validity of sacrifice).

> *You are not completely loving or freeing*
> *another person if you sacrifice an*
> *aspect of your being for them.*

To make a sacrifice for someone is to take away their power, their choice, and their right of creation.

To sacrifice yourself for another person is to live someone else's life rather than your own.

To sacrifice is to play the martyr.

No matter what the short-term benefits may outwardly be, to make a sacrifice is to create a future moment in your embodied experience when you will take back that power and retrieve whatever it is you have sacrificed.

CLARIFICATIONS & REFLECTIONS

Although we may feel that the sacrifices we make for others come from a place of love, it is important to be aware of the opposing motivations within any sacrifice. This is not so you can chastise or feel bad about yourself but so you can gain a deeper understanding of the unconscious fears that may be operating within you.

Be aware when looking at patterns of sacrifice in your life— *including relationships with those who ask you to sacrifice on their behalf*—that aside from the expression of love, there is often the desire to bind two selves together through an idea of a debt being created. The desire to create a feeling of debt is the desire to translate an inner feeling of attachment into an outward circumstance. Release this idea by knowing you are not owed anything by those for whom you have sacrificed and that you do not owe anything to those who have made sacrifices for you.

*Release any beliefs in the validity
of debt to release sacrifice.*

Within the realization of our unity is the realization that there is no separation of self across which debt can exist (because you cannot be indebted to yourself).

No dream exists to be sacrificed.

There is no need for one person to fail so another can succeed.

There is no need for a system of debt in order for us to help each other or for there to be fairness.

There is no need to cause other people to feel indebted to you so that you can feel loved and cared for.

Have the courage and breadth of vision to see that you can love without any notion of sacrifice or the creation of debt. The realization that *'no one owes you anything'* will make you feel happier as you are no longer attached to the repayment of a debt.

To choose to only act in ways that do not require the creation of debt—*because you are acting from your joy rather than sacrifice*—will not only elevate your personal relationships but also clarify which are based on love, as opposed to being transactional — the ones based on *'what we can do for each other.'*

By releasing the idea of self-sacrifice, you can love with a level of clarity and non-attachment that is more fulfilling for both yourself and those you love.

.

ALONE VERSUS IN RELATIONSHIP

"I choose to release any belief that I need to be within a relationship to be happy or accomplish my goals."

The nature of individuality means that although being in a relationship may relieve feelings of alienation or loneliness, it does not resolve them. Unless you intend never to be alone—*which many attempt*—to resolve the feeling of loneliness, you must not be afraid to fully meet it inside yourself.

Embrace your feeling of being alone as a source of strength and independence.

Do not fear or run from the feeling of being alone; it is not the cause of any unhappiness or negativity you may feel. The power and potential of all that companionship can only arise when you have met, embraced, and transformed your fear of being alone.

Unless you know you can stand alone and flourish in this life, you cannot fully stand in union with another person because a part of your relationship will always be governed by your fear of being alone. In this state, you are separated from a part of yourself, and your fear will manifest through your choices.

> *To experience Unified Diversity—as*
> *well as realizing the unity of all life—*
> *you must embrace your singularity/*
> *your uniqueness/your diversity.*

Unified Diversity is the allowance of both unity and separation. This is to embrace *all that you are—instead of only the parts that feel connected—*because it is to realize that whatever feels disconnected is still you. To only love that which feels connected is to be within a dualistic viewpoint (because to perceive and divide *what does feels connected* from *what does not feel connected* is an action that can only arise within polarized perception).

> Only when you give up the search for another person to complete you will you find the completeness that arises from loving *all that you are.*

> Only when you find *the love that you seek* within you will you find its reflection out in the world.

This is the reflective nature of our reality. The *'dream relationship'* with another person is primarily birthed through having the dream relationship with yourself first. Until that is in place, all external relationships will only ever point you back to resolving your fear of being alone.

Only by releasing your need to be with another person is it possible for your relationship to be based on equality. If you are alone, love it. If you are in a relationship, love it. Neither of these states is the cause or cure of loneliness.

Transform your loneliness by loving
it. Love it by celebrating it.

There is nothing you cannot do on your own.

CLARIFICATIONS & REFLECTIONS

Any thought of *"I will be happy when ..."* is a statement that denies you happiness in the present moment. This is to deny that in every moment, you have the freedom to choose an empowering vantage point on your circumstances—*'the glass is half full'*—versus a disempowering vantage point—*'the glass is half empty.'*

There is no *'wrongness,'* shame, or need for regret in choosing a negative vantage point; it is a choice to live in a reality you feel unhappy about (as opposed to one for which you feel gratitude). The amount of resistance a person has to the idea they are *'choosing to be unhappy'* is proportionate to how much they feel a victim of their reality (as opposed to the creator of it).

Being alone and being in a relationship
are both qualities of the mortal experience
made possible by our individuality.

They are equal and valid choices.

To step out of dualistic perception is to cease to polarize qualities such that *'being alone is bad'* and *'being in a relationship is good.'* It is to surrender to both fully (with the understanding that *all that you do fully, you do equally).* For some, this is about opening themselves to the positive aspects of being alone. Conversely, for others, it is about releasing their attachment to the control of being alone and opening their hearts to the uncertainty of loving someone else.

Whatever dualistic quality it may be (*alone—together, happy— unhappy, ill—healthy, rich—poor*), the resolution lies in seeing the relative equality of both states. Only then can you choose between them in freedom, instead of from a state of fear.

Many people want to be in a relationship when they are alone. Then, when they are in a relationship—*even when it is going well*—they miss some of the freedoms they experienced when single. This is a form of self-sabotage through which a person continually diminishes their experience of the present moment. To recognize this behavior in yourself means you have already begun transforming it.

Relationships are good.

Being alone is good.

They are two sides of one coin and you can master both.

INFINITE KNOWING
& VICTIMHOOD

*"I choose to view reality through clarity
rather than personal agenda."*

To know anything, you must know it as being of
yourself (as to know anything is to know it is of *the
one consciousness)*. To wake up to the nature of reality
is to know that you know whatever you want to know. Access
your power to know by allowing the feeling of *knowing that
you know.*

Although we cannot house all-knowing in our embodied
form, we each have access to omnipotence. You can know
anything you will allow yourself to know. And yet—*without
contradicting that infinite freedom*—you will find that if the
intention behind what you want to know is an attempt to
violate another person, then you cannot know because *'to
know,'* you must stand in your own power. This underscores
the immense power of intention coming from the heart,

which knows *all as one* (rather than the mind, which tends to polarize and divide your experience).

Creation is a heart-centered—not mental—focus of intention. To access your infinite knowing, you cannot be in a fight with the world. Your human self is a lens through which your spirit —*the one consciousness*—is looking at a reflection of itself. Your individuality is a self-defining lens (in our case, a human self-defining lens). As you learn more of yourself, you equally learn more about our shared world and your spirit.

In terms of perception, to view something through a tinted lens is the same as projecting the color of that tint onto it. This is called *'perceptual projection.'* To not know yourself is to not know the world (because you are unable to differentiate yourself from it). You transpose that which you do not know as yourself onto your perception of reality.

> *You view reality through that which*
> *you are denying in yourself.*

This is the basis of perceptual projection and is something we all do to some extent within human form (no matter how *'clear'* you think you are). The portal to infinite choice is *being who you are*, and that is to allow the potential for anything to change. To know reality, you must know yourself, and you cannot do this if you view yourself through an agenda of what you want to see.

> To access the power to become any *'thing,'* you must first not be afraid to know the *'thing'* you currently are.

> To change any aspect of yourself, you must first know it.

> To fully know something is to allow yourself to be it.

You must first be what you are to then become
something else.

Through self-awareness and the acceptance of whatever
it is you currently perceive as limited about yourself, you
perceptually transform that limitation back into freedom
through knowing it was created *in freedom/from love*. Your life
is your chosen perception of life. Through self-awareness, you
can awaken to the infinite nature of existence.

CLARIFICATIONS & REFLECTIONS
At first, the teaching that *'you cannot know something that will
violate the free will of another'* seems to imply a limit to our
infinite ability to experience. This perception of limitation
arises when you believe that your freedom of will is separate
from the freedom of the will of others. This state of perception
allows for the possibility of wanting something that someone
else does not. While this is true from the embodied self's level
of consciousness—*which is within an illusion of limitation*—it is
not true at the level of consciousness of your spirit.

> *My spirit cannot want something
> different from your spirit because they
> are both the one consciousness.*

This is to realize that the experience of unity—*which is
intrinsic to spirit*—applies to the experience of will. The
collective spirit of humanity carries a singular intention
to *'know itself'* through the expression of *all that the one
consciousness is.* This unified intention both underlies and
informs your intention for this life.

Although your mortal self may personally experience a
difference of will from someone else, this can only occur
through a personally created experience of separation (rather

than a fundamental difference of will). This means you can experience the illusion of contradicting someone else's free will, but only through the delusion of separation (which is another way of saying *'through your wounded aspects')*.

In moments of contradiction or violation, both parties share a common intention — to confront their most wounded aspects. This shared intention stems from our innate desire for self-discovery. It is an expression of our collective aspiration to transform the wounded aspects of our mortal selves, which are often manifested in extreme experiences of inequality, injustice, polarization, or separation.

To understand us all as equal creators is to no longer be able to perceive yourself as a victim. If you believe an external force has power over you, it is not possible to know yourself as the creator of your reality (which is to know yourself as your spirit). A part of accepting this is seeing how past trauma has made you the person you are today (because if you love yourself *as you are*, you do not want to change the past that helped form you).

To the eyes of *spirit/'God'/the one consciousness, ALL ARE EQUAL.* Victims are not better people than abusers. Victims and abusers are within equally deep experiences of separation from their inner power (just in opposing ways). There is no concept of blame in this—*as that is a divisive, polarizing action* —just an incredibly deep recognition that we are all equal creators.

Blame only ever perpetuates the victim-abuser cycle. Abusers and victims both need love to end their negative, fear-based cycle of interaction.

THE PERCEPTUAL
CURTAIN OF REALITY

*"I choose to meet myself through
spontaneity and inconsistency."*

T he answer that your heart seeks cannot be contained
in some definition or outward thing alone — it is a
feeling, and feelings are something that words can
only point to. What you seek is beyond definition, but *'beyond
definition'* is not beyond experience.

*The experience you seek will be yours
whenever you are ready to pull back
the curtain that currently stops
you from seeing your spirit.*

To pull back this curtain is to look beyond the comfort zone of
who you have been and what you have known. This is to open
yourself more deeply than ever before as to the potential of
your consciousness.

To meet your spirit, you must step beyond the limits that have defined your human self. This is to step beyond its patterns of behavior, thinking, emotional reactions, and polarized perception. These patterns are more fundamentally and descriptively what you are as a human being than even the solidity of your physical body.

Do not fear seeing the repeating patterns that underlie your human self. By doing this, you will discover the freedom of no longer conforming to the patterns you have known. You will discover the freedom of being *inconsistent* and you will meet *the unknown self* that arises beyond the experience of *the self that is known.*

> *To meet the unknown self is to*
> *change the known self.*

Surprise yourself. Allow yourself to be surprised. Discover the joy of surprise in yourself. Leave prior conceptions of yourself through the allowance of spontaneity. The comfort of a consistent self-chosen definition is a limitation of the past. The present is consistently inconsistent. To be in *'the Now'* is to be something different—*something fresh*—every day.

Being this inconsistent, spontaneous version of yourself will tell you more about what you essentially are than any mentally constructed pinnacle of truth arrived at through the refinement of *mental patterns/knowledge.*

> *Idealism blinds people from seeing*
> *beyond the mental.*

The intention of your spirit is pre-definition — pre-language and pre-conceptualization. What you essentially are is pre-Earth and pre-mortality.

Your human self is not what you are;
it is you exploring what you are.

Your spirit created the curtain of definition—*the veil of forgetting that leaves a focus*—that you experience your human self through. Look through the curtain of your *unconsciousness/forgetting* and you will meet yourself as the architect of your reality's definitions and cyclical patterns.

CLARIFICATIONS & REFLECTIONS
Within human form, we marvel at the complex diversity of what we are as a species and the magnitude of life expressed through the Earth. Our personalities are so different and varied that—*despite there being billions of us*—we still feel unique.

Layers upon layers—and layers within
layers—of definition have built up and
evolved through the human experience.

It can be hard to imagine how this infinite complexity arose out of what is seen to be a state of infinite simplicity (unity). See how the diverse complexity of the human experience allows for a greater feeling of separation and, by extension, the individuality we so treasure. The height of this complexity correlates to the depth of *individuality/separation* we have created through the human experience from which we are now perceptively returning.

Although this return is represented by an outward experience, it is a perceptual journey ... a journey through the curtain of definition we live within to the state of perception of our spirit. Through knowing your spirit, you are capable of seeing how every single human being is *the one consciousness* (God) experiencing itself through many diverse aspects (states of definition).

Moving towards your spirit's state of perception can initially feel like seeing yourself in a reduced way (partly because of how the individuality you have been identified with is seen to be a temporary form). Much of the complexity of your human experience arises through relatively simple patterns. Because of how something this complex can be accurately described through repeating patterns, this can feel like having something taken away from you. However, if you do not go into resistance, if you can accept and adapt to the changes, the next step—*that automatically arises from seeing these patterns* —is to intuitively see how to step beyond the aspects of these patterns with which you feel the least resonance.

> *To see through the illusion of separation is to lose some of the depth of your individuality.*

This happens because you are becoming more conscious of your wider nature and are less focused on your mortality. This is to meet yourself as the creator of all the patterns you have known yourself through as an individual.

> *Do not fear seeing repeated patterns inside of you.*

THE MASTERY OF FEAR

*"I choose not let what I fear lead me to
not choose what excites me most."*

U nderstanding that fear is not an external force but a
feeling of resistance is a powerful realization. It
incorporates a myriad of emotions and is often
triggered by external events. However, these events are not
the cause of the fear — they are external reflections of what
you are resistant to (and tell you something about yourself).
This understanding empowers you to meet the feeling of fear
as a powerful signpost to the aspects of reality that you have
resistance towards.

*Because fear is created by unconsciousness, all
fear is—at some level—a fear of the unknown.*

Instead of approaching the unknown with fear, meet it as a
reflection of the aspects of you that you have not yet felt ready
to meet.

*The mastery of fear arises from the acceptance
that there are no experiences of fear except
that which we create for ourselves.*

To explore your deepest fears is to explore the most
unconscious aspects of yourself. Trust in the chosen face of
your fear and you will be approaching its resolution from
an empowered standpoint. You will know when you have
finished exploring it because, when you stand in the breadth
of this knowing, you will no longer fear it.

*To live in fear is to be dominated by that
fear in such a way that you find yourself
unable to not include it in your focus.*

To be fearless is not to never feel fear—*as that is a part of being
human)*—it is to not be controlled by your fears. This means
no longer making fear-based choices by avoiding or trying
to control what you fear. *To be fearless is to choose what most
excites you without regard for what you fear.*

*The feeling of fear distorts the feeling of
guidance that our emotions offer.*

Fear not your fear — it is your freedom disguised as mental
doubt. This is to see the way in which your fear is your
freedom if you are willing to step through the change in
perception that it represents.

Instead of seeing fear as a *'bad thing,'* someone who has
mastered fear knows that the sheer strength of a profound
fear is an asset of feeling that reflects the potential for you to
open to a new reality by stepping through the experience of
facing and transforming it.

Meet your fear to more fully meet yourself.

Know thyself to know there is nothing to fear.

When you do not fear fear, you will cease to create with it. Walk through your fears to discover why you created them. This will reveal them as carefully crafted gateways of self-empowerment for you to potentially explore in this life.

CLARIFICATIONS & REFLECTIONS
Fear is the fear of feeling something. We do not fear external *'things'* — we fear what they may cause us to feel. To be a master of fear is to be a master of feeling, as it is to know there is nothing you are incapable of feeling. Feelings only ever have the power to temporarily consume you while you integrate their message of change.

No feeling has the power to destroy you.

Open yourself to experience feeling as being a courageous act. Feeling is the choice to be vulnerable and meet the aspects of yourself that most challenge you. By doing so, you meet these challenges at an emotional level, fully embracing what you have feared. This process of vulnerability is a powerful catalyst for personal growth, as it allows you to realize that the only *'things'* you will ever meet in life are more reflections of yourself ... more ways to *'know thyself.'*

To allow your vulnerability is the choice to be proud of your ability to show vulnerability and model it as a strength. This redefines strength as the ability to be open and transparent through the allowance of vulnerability.

If you wish to flex this muscle, invite change into your life around which you feel the greatest combination of fear and excitement. Seek experiences where you feel vulnerable. And then, when you feel that fear, relish exploring it, instead of perceiving it as a problem.

> *At the heart of your vulnerability*
> *is freedom—an unexpressed*
> *aspect of yourself—that you have*
> *been afraid of integrating.*

To feel and meet this freedom is to integrate that aspect. Approach your feelings of vulnerability with an open heart. Bask in its fiery energy as it flows through your body and destroys outdated fear-based patterns. Allow yourself to be changed by these feelings to meet a deeper experience of being embodied.

To awaken to your spirit is to know you are connected to everything, and that means, if you wish to experience the reality of that connection, you are open to feeling everything.

> *Feel everything to know thyself.*

Limiting and protecting your feelings limits your ability to feel and be. A heart that is truly open has no fear of feeling. A heart that knows freedom is equally open to feeling devastation and loss as it is to feeling love.

THE PHYSICAL VERSUS
THE NON-PHYSICAL

"I choose to experience the equality of the non-physical and the physical and thereby the equality of my spirit and human self."

Death and awakening are the same in that they both are an opening to the wider state of reality. Awakening is a transformative experience, a journey of self-discovery that inspires us to see the world in a new light. It is experienced through realizations that cause the meaning of everything to change — and yet, outwardly, the world continues in the same way it always has.

Our transformation in perception at death is both profound and revelatory, and yet, what you are at the most essential level (your spirit) remains the same. Although what outwardly defines you in this reality has no overt presence in the non-physical, what you most essentially are continues.

Just as our non-physical self continues beyond our physical death, so too does the spirit of division continue. Division, as we perceive it, does not exist within the perception of the unified consciousness (because it requires polarized perception). However, in the same way that our mortal form is a translation of our spirit, the experience of division is equally a translation of *'something.'* When we die, just as we directly experience our spirit—*instead of experiencing it as a translation*—we also directly experience what that division is a translation of.

> *Our physical reality is not completely different from our spiritual reality; it is an alternate translation of it.*
>
> *Death is a change of perspective.*

When we die, what we essentially are continues. We are just expressed through a different perception—*and projection* —of reality. Although death is the release of our outer circumstances, there is nothing that we have been exploring that is *'escaped.'* If you have always felt the need to escape, you will continue to experience what this need was reflecting after death because it will be expressed within your intention— *formed in the non-physical*—for physical life.

What you are within physicality is the physical expression and translation of what you are in spirit. You can step out of your physical expression but you remain what you are (just not expressed in physical form).

This is the realization of the equality of life and death, the physical and the non-physical, and the mortal and the immortal. It is the teaching *'as above, so below.'*

The human reality and the non-physical are not as different as we believe because they are both reflections of the one consciousness.

However, even though *'above'* is not better than *'below,'* to awaken to its existence is one of the most incredible experiences within creation.

CLARIFICATIONS & REFLECTIONS

The separation we perceive between the non-physical—*the reality of our eternal spirit*—and the physical—*the reality of our mortal body*—is an illusion. To awaken to our spirit is to awaken to our nature beyond the physical, but that is not a denunciation of the physical. Once you have awoken to your wider nature, you will realize the way in which your physicality is as one with your spirit. And in death—*when you step from the expression of your body*—you will experience the choice of your spirit—*the one consciousness*—for this physical life.

At a collective level, we have a deep-seated need for our physical death to be the end of all pain and resistance.

Many people are attached to the idea that the afterlife is a utopia — the entering of which will instantly resolve all our struggles and leave us wanting for nothing. This belief is a comfort blanket that has arisen out of a need to soothe our mind from the mental challenges it faces in finding meaning to align with (particularly in a reality created by polarized perception).

The illusion of reality is a translation of something we each directly experience at death (instead of indirectly experiencing it through the translation of a human life). Beneath the many diverse hopes we have for the afterlife is the shared idea that when we die and leave our physical form, everything will change. However, just as the rainbow is a translation of *the one consciousness* into color, the human body is a translation of *the one consciousness* into separation. So, even though what we call color and separation are not perceptible from within the unified state of consciousness, they are still a translation of something that does exist within the non-physical.

This points to what continues beyond death within you (that which we call *'our spirit'*). Even though every outer thing does change at death—*the experience of everything changes*—we each also experience the level at which *nothing changes.* This is because all those outer things are diverse translations of the same non-physical thing—*our spirit*—that continues to exist regardless of whether or not we are embodied.

The ideas that nothing changes and everything changes both contain truth because they describe the reflection and the reflected.

> *Do not fear everything*
> *changing when you die.*
>
> *Do not fear nothing*
> *changing when you die.*

ABOUT THE AUTHOR

Story Waters is a gnostic writer and speaker (AKA channeler). In 2003, he sat up in bed one morning and wrote out the basis of his first book, *The Messiah Seed.* In 2013, he began communicating with Seth, who, along with Jane Roberts, opened Story to the unified nature of our wider, eternal state of consciousness. By fearlessly peeling back the layers of his gnostic process, Story discovered Seth to be his chosen interface for the living library of all selves (AKA The Akashic Records).

"Through developing my intuition/inner guidance, I have learned to access the collective body of infinite consciousness we all birth from. This is not a special gift. The gnostic process is an altogether

'normal' level of perception. Everyone accesses it at a subconscious level. How conscious you become of this connection is determined by how much you focus on it." — Story Waters.

Story was born in Brighton, England, in 1972. He now lives in upstate New York with his husband and visionary artist, Roger Hanson, and their dog, Ghost. Story's complete writing is currently being released through Amazon and his live recordings through audiobook. *'No Religion: Consciousness Creates Reality: The Book of Introductions'* is a great place to start and is available as both an illustrated text and an audiobook.

"You are eternal consciousness in human form. Your spirit is an infinite state of consciousness that knows it is far more than the individuated, temporary, mortal self you are currently experiencing. Through its wider focus/perceptual aperture, your spirit knows it is connected to everything in existence. The human experience is a game that infinite consciousness plays with itself, where it suppresses its infinite multidirectional perception by looking through a pair of binoculars. It then pretends that what it sees through this attenuation of perception is separate from it and is the one physical reality in existence." — Story Waters.

BOOKS & RECORDINGS
BY STORY WATERS

You Are God. Get Over It!: Expanded 2nd edition

You Are Human. Get Over It!

You have a place/purpose in this world.

The Time Weaver's Guide: Expand Your Temporal Focus.

Human by Design: The Power and Artistry of Choice.

Unconventional Belief Systems & the Conscious Universe.

The Book of Introductions.

Abundance and the Cycles of Life.

I Am Not Separate.

The Awakening Codes.

Being Without Protection.

Practical Channeling and Intuition Course.

Creating Timeless Flow.

The One Self Teachings.

Reality Is a Donut: A Metaphysical Masterclass.

Perspectives with Seth, Volumes 1,2, & 3.

Shards of Light.

The Gnostic Writer Article Collection.

The Relationship Elevator

The Bridge of Consciousness

The One Self Teachings

The Passion Activation

These books, eBooks, and recordings are primarily available through Amazon (which includes Audible).